50 Gourmet Recipes for Home

By: Kelly Johnson

Table of Contents

Appetizers:
- Baked Brie with Fig and Walnut Compote
- Crispy Polenta Bites with Goat Cheese and Sun-Dried Tomatoes
- Scallop Ceviche with Mango and Avocado
- Truffle and Parmesan Arancini
- Smoked Salmon and Cucumber Rolls
- Gruyere and Mushroom Tartlets
- Prosciutto-Wrapped Asparagus Bundles

Soups:
- Lobster Bisque with Cognac
- Creamy Truffle Cauliflower Soup
- Lentil and Saffron Soup with Greek Yogurt Drizzle
- Roasted Red Pepper and Goat Cheese Soup
- Truffle-Infused Wild Mushroom Soup
- Chilled Avocado and Cucumber Gazpacho
- White Bean and Truffle Oil Soup

Salads:
- Watercress, Blood Orange and Pomegranate Salad
- Pear, Gouda and Candied Pecan Salad with White Balsamic Vinaigrette

Main Courses - Seafood:
- Seared Scallops with Lemon Beurre Blanc
- Pan-Roasted Halibut with Saffron Cream Sauce
- Lobster Risotto with Truffle Oil
- Citrus and Herb Grilled Shrimp Skewers
- Salmon en Papillote with Dill and Lemon
- Miso-Glazed Black Cod with Sesame Ginger Broccolini
- Cioppino (Italian Seafood Stew) with Garlic Bread

Main Courses - Meat:
- Filet Mignon with Red Wine Reduction
- Duck Confit with Orange Gastrique
- Herb-Crusted Rack of Lamb with Mint Pesto
- Coq au Vin
- Coffee-Rubbed Lamb Chops with Rosemary Demi-Glace
- Dijon and Herb-Crusted Pork Tenderloin with Apple Compote

Pasta and Risotto:
- Veal Saltimbocca with Sage and Prosciutto
- Lobster and Champagne Risotto
- Truffle Butter Gnocchi
- Wild Mushroom and Fontina Ravioli with Brown Butter Sauce
- Pappardelle with Braised Short Rib Ragu
- Lemon and Shrimp Scampi Linguine

Vegetarian:
- Eggplant Parmesan Tower with Fresh Tomato Sauce
- Quinoa-Stuffed Bell Peppers with Feta and Spinach
- Butternut Squash and Sage Risotto
- Wild Mushroom and Spinach Stuffed Portobello Mushrooms
- Vegetarian Moussaka

Side Dishes:
- Truffle Mashed Potatoes
- Grilled Asparagus with Lemon Zest and Parmesan
- Cauliflower Gratin with Gruyere
- Roasted Brussels Sprouts with Balsamic Glaze and Bacon
- Wild Rice Pilaf with Pomegranate Seeds and Pistachios

Appetizers

Baked Brie with Fig and Walnut Compote

Ingredients:

- 1 round of Brie cheese (about 8 ounces)
- 1/2 cup dried figs, chopped
- 1/4 cup walnuts, chopped
- 2 tablespoons honey
- 1 tablespoon balsamic vinegar
- 1 tablespoon water
- 1 teaspoon fresh rosemary, chopped
- Crackers or baguette slices for serving

Instructions:

Preheat Oven:
- Preheat your oven to 350°F (175°C).

Prepare Brie:
- Place the Brie round on a parchment-lined baking sheet.

Make Compote:
- In a small saucepan, combine chopped dried figs, chopped walnuts, honey, balsamic vinegar, and water.
- Simmer over medium heat, stirring occasionally, until the mixture thickens and the figs become soft (about 5-7 minutes).
- Stir in fresh rosemary and remove from heat.

Top Brie:
- Spoon the fig and walnut compote over the top of the Brie.

Bake:
- Bake the Brie in the preheated oven for 10-12 minutes, or until the Brie is soft and gooey.

Serve:
- Carefully transfer the baked Brie to a serving platter. You can leave it on the parchment paper for an easy transfer.
- Serve immediately with crackers or baguette slices.

Enjoy:
- Enjoy the gooey, warm Baked Brie with Fig and Walnut Compote!

This appetizer is perfect for entertaining guests or adding a touch of elegance to your gathering. The combination of creamy Brie, sweet figs, crunchy walnuts, and the hint of rosemary creates a sophisticated and delicious flavor profile.

Crispy Polenta Bites with Goat Cheese and Sun-Dried Tomatoes

Ingredients:

- 1 cup instant polenta
- 4 cups water
- 1 teaspoon salt
- 1/2 cup grated Parmesan cheese
- 2 tablespoons butter
- 4 ounces goat cheese, crumbled
- 1/4 cup sun-dried tomatoes, finely chopped
- Salt and pepper to taste
- Olive oil for frying
- Fresh basil leaves for garnish (optional)

Instructions:

Cook Polenta:
- In a medium saucepan, bring 4 cups of water to a boil. Add salt and slowly whisk in the instant polenta.
- Reduce the heat to low and continue to whisk until the polenta thickens, about 5 minutes.
- Stir in the grated Parmesan cheese and butter until fully incorporated.

Season and Shape:
- Season the polenta with salt and pepper to taste. Spread the polenta onto a parchment-lined baking sheet to cool and set, about 1/2 inch thick. Allow it to cool completely.

Cut into Bites:
- Once the polenta has cooled and set, use a cookie cutter or knife to cut it into bite-sized rounds or squares.

Prepare Filling:
- In a small bowl, mix crumbled goat cheese with finely chopped sun-dried tomatoes.

Assemble Bites:
- Place a small amount of the goat cheese and sun-dried tomato mixture on top of each polenta bite.

Pan-Fry:
- Heat olive oil in a skillet over medium-high heat. Once hot, add the polenta bites and fry until crispy and golden brown on each side, about 2-3 minutes per side.

Serve:
- Remove the crispy polenta bites from the skillet and place them on a serving platter.
- Garnish with fresh basil leaves if desired.

Enjoy:
- Serve the Crispy Polenta Bites with Goat Cheese and Sun-Dried Tomatoes as a delightful appetizer or snack.

These bites offer a combination of creamy goat cheese, sweet sun-dried tomatoes, and the crispy texture of polenta. They make for an elegant and flavorful addition to any gathering.

Scallop Ceviche with Mango and Avocado

Ingredients:

- 1 pound fresh scallops, cleaned and thinly sliced
- 1/2 cup freshly squeezed lime juice
- 1/4 cup freshly squeezed lemon juice
- 1/4 cup freshly squeezed orange juice
- 1 ripe mango, peeled, pitted, and diced
- 1 ripe avocado, peeled, pitted, and diced
- 1 small red onion, finely chopped
- 1 jalapeño pepper, seeded and finely chopped
- 1/4 cup fresh cilantro, chopped
- Salt and pepper to taste
- Tortilla chips or crackers for serving

Instructions:

Prepare Scallop Marinade:
- In a glass or ceramic bowl, combine the lime juice, lemon juice, and orange juice. This will serve as the marinade for the scallops.

Marinate Scallops:
- Add the thinly sliced scallops to the marinade, ensuring they are fully submerged. Cover the bowl with plastic wrap and refrigerate for about 30 minutes to 1 hour. The acidity of the citrus juices will "cook" the scallops.

Prepare Mango, Avocado, and Other Ingredients:
- Meanwhile, dice the mango and avocado into small cubes. Finely chop the red onion, jalapeño pepper, and cilantro.

Combine Ingredients:
- Once the scallops have marinated, drain off the excess marinade. Transfer the scallops to a clean bowl.
- Add the diced mango, avocado, red onion, jalapeño pepper, and chopped cilantro to the bowl with the scallops. Gently toss to combine.

Season:
- Season the ceviche with salt and pepper to taste. Adjust the seasoning as needed.

Chill:
- Cover the bowl with plastic wrap and refrigerate the ceviche for an additional 15-30 minutes to allow the flavors to meld together.

Serve:

- Serve the scallop ceviche with mango and avocado in chilled bowls or martini glasses. Garnish with additional cilantro if desired.
- Serve with tortilla chips or crackers on the side for scooping up the ceviche.

Enjoy:

- Enjoy the refreshing and vibrant flavors of scallop ceviche with mango and avocado as a delightful appetizer or light meal!

This scallop ceviche is perfect for entertaining guests or enjoying as a refreshing snack on a hot day. The combination of tender scallops, sweet mango, creamy avocado, and zesty citrus is sure to impress your taste buds.

Truffle and Parmesan Arancini

Ingredients:

- 2 cups Arborio rice
- 1/2 cup dry white wine
- 6 cups chicken or vegetable broth, kept warm
- 1 small onion, finely chopped
- 2 tablespoons truffle oil
- 1 cup freshly grated Parmesan cheese
- Salt and pepper to taste
- 2 large eggs, beaten
- 2 cups breadcrumbs
- Vegetable oil for frying
- Marinara sauce for serving

Instructions:

Prepare Risotto:
- In a large pan, sauté the chopped onion in a bit of olive oil until translucent. Add the Arborio rice and cook for a couple of minutes until lightly toasted.
- Pour in the white wine and allow it to evaporate. Begin adding the warm broth, one ladle at a time, stirring frequently. Continue this process until the rice is cooked and has a creamy consistency.

Season and Flavor:
- Season the risotto with salt and pepper to taste. Stir in truffle oil and freshly grated Parmesan cheese. Adjust the seasoning and truffle flavor according to your preference.

Cool Risotto:
- Allow the risotto to cool completely. You can spread it out on a baking sheet to speed up the cooling process.

Shape Arancini:
- Once the risotto is cooled, take a portion in your hands and shape it into a ball. Press a small indentation into the center and place a small piece of mozzarella in the center. Reform the ball to encase the cheese.

Coat in Breadcrumbs:
- Dip each arancini ball into the beaten eggs and then roll it in breadcrumbs until evenly coated.

Heat Oil:

- In a deep fryer or a large, deep skillet, heat vegetable oil to 350°F (175°C).

Fry Arancini:
- Carefully place the arancini in the hot oil and fry until golden brown on all sides. This should take about 3-4 minutes. Do not overcrowd the pan; fry in batches if necessary.

Drain and Serve:
- Once golden brown, remove the arancini with a slotted spoon and place them on a plate lined with paper towels to drain any excess oil.

Serve with Marinara Sauce:
- Serve the truffle and Parmesan arancini hot with a side of marinara sauce for dipping.

Enjoy:
- Enjoy the rich and flavorful Truffle and Parmesan Arancini as a delicious appetizer or a delightful party snack!

These arancini are a perfect combination of creamy risotto, the earthy aroma of truffle oil, and the savory kick of Parmesan cheese, all encased in a crispy breadcrumb shell.

Smoked Salmon and Cucumber Rolls

Ingredients:

- 1 large cucumber
- 4 ounces smoked salmon
- 4 ounces cream cheese, softened
- 2 tablespoons fresh dill, chopped
- 1 tablespoon capers (optional)
- 1 tablespoon lemon juice
- Salt and pepper to taste
- Toothpicks or small skewers

Instructions:

Prepare the Cucumber:
- Wash the cucumber and cut thin, lengthwise slices using a mandoline or a vegetable peeler. Lay the slices on a clean kitchen towel to absorb excess moisture.

Prepare the Filling:
- In a bowl, mix the softened cream cheese, chopped fresh dill, capers (if using), and lemon juice. Season with salt and pepper to taste.

Assemble the Rolls:
- Take a cucumber slice and spread a thin layer of the cream cheese mixture over it.
- Place a slice of smoked salmon on top of the cream cheese.

Roll Up:
- Carefully roll the cucumber slice with the cream cheese and smoked salmon into a tight spiral.

Secure with Toothpick:
- Secure the roll with a toothpick or small skewer to hold it in place. Repeat the process with the remaining cucumber slices.

Chill:
- Place the rolled-up smoked salmon and cucumber bites in the refrigerator for about 15-20 minutes to chill and firm up.

Slice and Serve:
- Once chilled, remove the toothpicks and slice the rolls into bite-sized pieces.

Garnish (Optional):
- Garnish with additional dill or a sprinkle of capers if desired.

Serve:
- Arrange the smoked salmon and cucumber rolls on a serving platter and serve immediately.

Enjoy:
- Enjoy these light and flavorful Smoked Salmon and Cucumber Rolls as an elegant appetizer or part of a brunch spread!

These rolls are not only visually appealing but also offer a delightful combination of cool cucumber, creamy cheese, and the distinct flavor of smoked salmon. They make for a sophisticated addition to any gathering.

Gruyere and Mushroom Tartlets

Ingredients:

For the Tartlet Shells:

- 1 sheet of frozen puff pastry, thawed
- All-purpose flour for dusting

For the Mushroom Filling:

- 1 tablespoon olive oil
- 1 small onion, finely chopped
- 8 ounces cremini or button mushrooms, finely chopped
- 2 cloves garlic, minced
- Salt and pepper to taste
- 1 tablespoon fresh thyme leaves

For the Gruyere Custard:

- 1 cup Gruyere cheese, shredded
- 1/2 cup whole milk
- 2 large eggs
- Salt and pepper to taste
- Nutmeg (optional, for a hint of nutty flavor)

Instructions:

Preheat Oven:
- Preheat your oven to 375°F (190°C).

Prepare Tartlet Shells:
- On a lightly floured surface, roll out the puff pastry sheet to smooth out any creases. Using a round cookie cutter or a glass, cut out circles from the puff pastry and press them into the cups of a mini muffin tin.

Prick with a Fork:
- Prick the bottom of each tartlet shell with a fork to prevent puffing during baking.

Bake Tartlet Shells:
- Bake the tartlet shells in the preheated oven for about 10 minutes or until they are lightly golden. Remove from the oven and set aside.

Prepare Mushroom Filling:
- In a skillet, heat olive oil over medium heat. Add chopped onions and sauté until they become translucent.
- Add minced garlic and chopped mushrooms to the skillet. Cook until the mushrooms release their moisture and become golden brown. Season with salt, pepper, and fresh thyme.

Make Gruyere Custard:
- In a bowl, whisk together shredded Gruyere, whole milk, eggs, salt, pepper, and a pinch of nutmeg if using.

Assemble Tartlets:
- Spoon the mushroom filling into each pre-baked tartlet shell.
- Pour the Gruyere custard mixture over the mushroom filling, filling each tartlet.

Bake Again:
- Bake the assembled tartlets in the oven for an additional 15-20 minutes or until the custard is set and the tops are golden brown.

Cool and Serve:
- Allow the tartlets to cool slightly before removing them from the muffin tin. Serve warm.

Enjoy:
- Enjoy these Gruyere and Mushroom Tartlets as a savory and elegant appetizer!

These tartlets offer a delightful combination of flaky puff pastry, earthy mushrooms, and the rich, nutty flavor of Gruyere cheese. They are sure to impress your guests at any gathering.

Prosciutto-Wrapped Asparagus Bundles

Ingredients:

- 1 bunch of fresh asparagus spears, tough ends trimmed
- Olive oil for drizzling
- Salt and black pepper to taste
- 8-10 slices of prosciutto
- Balsamic glaze for drizzling (optional)
- Toothpicks

Instructions:

Preheat Oven:
- Preheat your oven to 400°F (200°C).

Prepare Asparagus:
- Wash and trim the tough ends of the asparagus spears. If the spears are thick, you can peel them lightly to ensure tenderness.

Season Asparagus:
- Drizzle the asparagus spears with olive oil and season with salt and black pepper. Toss them to coat evenly.

Bundle Asparagus:
- Take 4-5 asparagus spears and bundle them together. Wrap a slice of prosciutto around each bundle, covering the bottom of the asparagus spears.

Secure with Toothpicks:
- Use toothpicks to secure the prosciutto to the asparagus, ensuring they stay together during cooking.

Arrange on Baking Sheet:
- Place the prosciutto-wrapped asparagus bundles on a baking sheet lined with parchment paper.

Bake:
- Bake in the preheated oven for about 10-12 minutes or until the asparagus is tender and the prosciutto is crispy.

Optional Broil:
- If you prefer, you can broil the bundles for an additional 1-2 minutes to crisp up the prosciutto further. Keep a close eye to prevent burning.

Drizzle with Balsamic Glaze (Optional):
- Once out of the oven, you can drizzle the prosciutto-wrapped asparagus bundles with balsamic glaze for an extra touch of flavor.

Serve:
- Remove the toothpicks before serving. Arrange the bundles on a serving platter.

Enjoy:
- Enjoy these Prosciutto-Wrapped Asparagus Bundles as a delicious and visually appealing appetizer or side dish!

This dish combines the crispiness of prosciutto with the freshness of asparagus, creating a delightful contrast of textures and flavors. It's a perfect addition to any special meal or gathering.

Soups

Lobster Bisque with Cognac

Ingredients:

- 2 lobsters (about 1 1/2 to 2 pounds each)
- 1/2 cup unsalted butter
- 1 onion, finely chopped
- 1 carrot, finely chopped
- 2 celery stalks, finely chopped
- 3 cloves garlic, minced
- 1/4 cup all-purpose flour
- 2 tablespoons tomato paste
- 1/2 cup cognac
- 4 cups fish or lobster stock
- 2 cups heavy cream
- 1 teaspoon paprika
- Salt and black pepper to taste
- Chopped fresh chives or parsley for garnish

Instructions:

Prepare Lobsters:

- Bring a large pot of salted water to a boil. Cook the lobsters for about 8-10 minutes until they turn red. Remove from the pot and let them cool. Once cooled, crack the lobster shells and extract the meat. Reserve the shells for later.

Make Lobster Stock:

- In the same pot, melt 2 tablespoons of butter and sauté the lobster shells, onion, carrot, celery, and garlic until they become aromatic. Add fish or lobster stock and bring to a simmer. Let it simmer for about 30-45 minutes. Strain the stock, discarding the solids.

Prepare Lobster Meat:

- Chop the lobster meat into bite-sized pieces.

Make Roux:

- In a large pot, melt the remaining butter over medium heat. Add the flour and stir continuously to create a roux. Cook the roux for a few minutes until it turns a light golden brown.

Add Tomato Paste and Cognac:

- Stir in the tomato paste and cook for an additional 2 minutes. Add the cognac, scraping any bits from the bottom of the pot.

Add Stock and Cream:

- Gradually whisk in the lobster stock, followed by heavy cream. Bring the mixture to a gentle simmer.

Season:

- Season the bisque with paprika, salt, and black pepper. Adjust the seasoning to your taste.

Add Lobster Meat:

- Add the chopped lobster meat to the bisque and let it simmer for an additional 5-7 minutes, allowing the flavors to meld.

Finish with Cognac:

- Just before serving, stir in an additional splash of cognac to enhance the flavor.

Serve:

- Ladle the lobster bisque into bowls, garnish with chopped fresh chives or parsley, and serve hot.

Enjoy:

- Enjoy this rich and decadent Lobster Bisque with Cognac as a luxurious appetizer or part of a special meal!

This lobster bisque is sure to impress with its velvety texture and the deep, savory flavor of cognac. It's a delightful treat for seafood lovers.

Creamy Truffle Cauliflower Soup

Ingredients:

- 1 large cauliflower, chopped into florets
- 1 onion, finely chopped
- 2 cloves garlic, minced
- 2 tablespoons butter
- 4 cups vegetable or chicken broth
- 1 cup heavy cream
- 1 tablespoon truffle oil
- Salt and pepper to taste
- Fresh chives or parsley for garnish (optional)
- Truffle slices or truffle salt for topping (optional)

Instructions:

Sauté Vegetables:

- In a large pot, melt the butter over medium heat. Add the chopped onion and garlic, sautéing until softened.

Add Cauliflower:

- Add the cauliflower florets to the pot. Stir and cook for a few minutes until they begin to soften.

Pour in Broth:

- Pour in the vegetable or chicken broth, ensuring it covers the cauliflower. Bring the mixture to a simmer and cook until the cauliflower is tender.

Blend Soup:

- Use an immersion blender to puree the soup until smooth. If you don't have an immersion blender, carefully transfer the mixture to a blender and blend in batches.

Add Cream and Truffle Oil:

- Return the pureed soup to the pot over low heat. Stir in the heavy cream and truffle oil. Season with salt and pepper to taste. Allow the soup to warm through.

Adjust Consistency:

- If the soup is too thick, you can add more broth or cream to reach your desired consistency.

Serve:

- Ladle the creamy truffle cauliflower soup into bowls.

Garnish:

- Garnish with fresh chives or parsley, and for an extra touch of luxury, you can top each serving with truffle slices or a sprinkle of truffle salt.

Enjoy:

- Serve the Creamy Truffle Cauliflower Soup hot and savor the rich and earthy flavors!

This soup is a delightful combination of creamy cauliflower goodness and the luxurious essence of truffle oil. It's a perfect starter for an elegant dinner or a comforting dish for a cozy evening.

Lentil and Saffron Soup with Greek Yogurt Drizzle

Ingredients:

For the Soup:

- 1 cup dried green or brown lentils, rinsed and drained
- 1 large onion, finely chopped
- 2 carrots, peeled and diced
- 2 celery stalks, diced
- 3 cloves garlic, minced
- 1 teaspoon ground cumin
- 1 teaspoon ground coriander
- 1/2 teaspoon ground turmeric
- 1/4 teaspoon saffron threads
- 6 cups vegetable or chicken broth
- 2 bay leaves
- Salt and pepper to taste
- 2 tablespoons olive oil

For the Greek Yogurt Drizzle:

- 1/2 cup Greek yogurt
- 1 tablespoon fresh lemon juice
- 1 tablespoon chopped fresh mint
- Salt and pepper to taste

Instructions:

Sauté Aromatics:

- In a large pot, heat olive oil over medium heat. Add chopped onions, carrots, celery, and minced garlic. Sauté until the vegetables are softened.

Add Lentils and Spices:

- Stir in the lentils, ground cumin, ground coriander, ground turmeric, and saffron threads. Cook for a couple of minutes to toast the spices.

Pour in Broth:

- Pour in the vegetable or chicken broth. Add bay leaves, salt, and pepper to taste. Bring the mixture to a boil, then reduce the heat to low, cover, and simmer until the lentils are tender.

Remove Bay Leaves:

- Once the lentils are cooked, remove the bay leaves.

Blend Soup (Optional):

- For a smoother texture, you can use an immersion blender to partially blend the soup. This step is optional, and you can leave the soup chunky if you prefer.

Prepare Greek Yogurt Drizzle:

- In a small bowl, whisk together Greek yogurt, fresh lemon juice, chopped mint, salt, and pepper.

Serve:

- Ladle the lentil and saffron soup into bowls. Drizzle a spoonful of the Greek yogurt mixture on top of each serving.

Garnish:

- Garnish with additional mint leaves if desired.

Enjoy:

- Enjoy this hearty and aromatic Lentil and Saffron Soup with the creamy Greek Yogurt Drizzle!

This soup combines the earthy flavors of lentils with the subtle warmth of saffron, and the Greek yogurt drizzle adds a tangy and refreshing element. It's a comforting and nutritious dish perfect for any time of the year.

Roasted Red Pepper and Goat Cheese Soup

Ingredients:

- 3 large red bell peppers, roasted, peeled, and chopped
- 1 onion, finely chopped
- 2 cloves garlic, minced
- 2 tablespoons olive oil
- 4 cups vegetable or chicken broth
- 1 potato, peeled and diced
- 1/2 cup goat cheese, crumbled
- 1/2 cup heavy cream
- Salt and black pepper to taste
- Fresh basil or chives for garnish (optional)

Instructions:

Roast Red Peppers:

- Preheat your oven broiler. Place whole red bell peppers on a baking sheet and broil, turning occasionally, until the skin is charred and blistered. Transfer the peppers to a bowl, cover with plastic wrap, and let them steam for about 10 minutes. Peel, seed, and chop the roasted peppers.

Sauté Aromatics:

- In a large pot, heat olive oil over medium heat. Add chopped onions and garlic, sautéing until softened.

Add Roasted Red Peppers:

- Add the roasted and chopped red peppers to the pot. Stir well.

Cook Potatoes:

- Add diced potatoes to the pot and cook for a few minutes.

Pour in Broth:
- Pour in the vegetable or chicken broth. Bring the mixture to a boil, then reduce the heat to low, cover, and simmer until the potatoes are tender.

Blend Soup:
- Use an immersion blender to puree the soup until smooth. If you don't have an immersion blender, carefully transfer the mixture to a blender and blend in batches.

Add Goat Cheese and Cream:
- Stir in crumbled goat cheese and heavy cream. Continue to cook over low heat until the goat cheese is melted and the soup is heated through.

Season:
- Season the soup with salt and black pepper to taste. Adjust the seasoning if needed.

Serve:
- Ladle the Roasted Red Pepper and Goat Cheese Soup into bowls.

Garnish:
- Garnish with fresh basil or chives if desired.

Enjoy:
- Enjoy the rich and velvety Roasted Red Pepper and Goat Cheese Soup as a comforting and flavorful appetizer or main course!

This soup is a wonderful combination of the smoky sweetness from the roasted red peppers and the creamy tanginess of goat cheese. It's a comforting dish that's perfect for cooler days.

Truffle-Infused Wild Mushroom Soup

Ingredients:

- 1 pound mixed wild mushrooms (such as shiitake, oyster, chanterelle), cleaned and sliced
- 1 onion, finely chopped
- 2 cloves garlic, minced
- 2 tablespoons butter
- 2 tablespoons olive oil
- 1/4 cup all-purpose flour
- 4 cups vegetable or chicken broth
- 1 cup heavy cream
- 1 tablespoon truffle oil
- Salt and black pepper to taste
- Fresh chives or parsley for garnish (optional)

Instructions:

Sauté Mushrooms:

- In a large pot, heat butter and olive oil over medium heat. Add chopped onions and garlic, sautéing until softened. Add sliced wild mushrooms and cook until they release their moisture and become golden brown.

Make Roux:

- Sprinkle flour over the mushrooms and stir well to create a roux. Cook for a few minutes to remove the raw taste of the flour.

Pour in Broth:

- Gradually pour in the vegetable or chicken broth while continuously stirring to avoid lumps. Bring the mixture to a simmer.

Simmer:

- Allow the soup to simmer for about 15-20 minutes, letting the flavors meld and the mushrooms become tender.

Blend Soup (Optional):

- For a smoother texture, you can use an immersion blender to partially blend the soup. This step is optional, and you can leave the soup chunky if you prefer.

Add Cream and Truffle Oil:

- Stir in the heavy cream and truffle oil. Season with salt and black pepper to taste. Allow the soup to warm through.

Adjust Consistency:

- If the soup is too thick, you can add more broth or cream to reach your desired consistency.

Serve:

- Ladle the Truffle-Infused Wild Mushroom Soup into bowls.

Garnish:

- Garnish with fresh chives or parsley if desired.

Enjoy:

- Enjoy the indulgent and aromatic Truffle-Infused Wild Mushroom Soup as a comforting and sophisticated appetizer or main course!

This soup is a celebration of the robust flavors of wild mushrooms complemented by the decadent truffle oil. It's a perfect dish for special occasions or when you want to treat yourself to a gourmet experience.

Chilled Avocado and Cucumber Gazpacho

Ingredients:

- 2 ripe avocados, peeled and diced
- 1 English cucumber, peeled and diced
- 1 green bell pepper, diced
- 1/2 red onion, diced
- 2 cloves garlic, minced
- 3 cups vegetable broth
- 1/4 cup fresh cilantro, chopped
- 1/4 cup fresh mint, chopped
- 1/4 cup fresh lime juice
- 2 tablespoons olive oil
- Salt and black pepper to taste
- Optional garnish: diced tomatoes, croutons, or additional herbs

Instructions:

Prepare Vegetables:

- Dice the avocados, cucumber, green bell pepper, and red onion. If you prefer a smoother soup, reserve a portion of the diced vegetables for garnish.

Blend Ingredients:

- In a blender or food processor, combine the diced avocados, cucumber, green bell pepper, red onion, minced garlic, vegetable broth, cilantro, mint, lime juice, and olive oil. Blend until smooth.

Season:

- Season the gazpacho with salt and black pepper to taste. Adjust the seasoning if needed.

Chill:

- Transfer the blended mixture to a large bowl and refrigerate for at least 2 hours to allow the flavors to meld and the soup to chill.

Serve:

- Ladle the Chilled Avocado and Cucumber Gazpacho into bowls.

Garnish (Optional):

- Garnish with diced tomatoes, croutons, or additional chopped herbs. If you reserved some diced vegetables, you can add them for a bit of texture.

Enjoy:

- Serve the chilled gazpacho and enjoy the cool, creamy goodness!

This gazpacho is a wonderful blend of creamy avocado, crisp cucumber, and vibrant herbs, creating a light and refreshing soup. It's a perfect starter or a light meal for hot summer days.

White Bean and Truffle Oil Soup

Ingredients:

- 2 cans (15 ounces each) white beans, drained and rinsed (or 3 cups cooked white beans)
- 1 onion, finely chopped
- 2 carrots, peeled and diced
- 2 celery stalks, diced
- 3 cloves garlic, minced
- 4 cups vegetable or chicken broth
- 2 bay leaves
- 1 teaspoon dried thyme
- Salt and black pepper to taste
- 2 tablespoons truffle oil
- Fresh parsley for garnish (optional)
- Grated Parmesan cheese for serving (optional)

Instructions:

Sauté Vegetables:

- In a large pot, heat olive oil over medium heat. Add chopped onions, carrots, celery, and minced garlic. Sauté until the vegetables are softened.

Add White Beans:

- Add the drained and rinsed white beans to the pot. Stir well to combine with the vegetables.

Pour in Broth:

- Pour in the vegetable or chicken broth. Add bay leaves and dried thyme. Bring the mixture to a boil.

Simmer:
- Reduce the heat to low, cover the pot, and let the soup simmer for about 15-20 minutes, allowing the flavors to meld and the vegetables to become tender.

Season:
- Season the soup with salt and black pepper to taste. Remove the bay leaves.

Blend Soup (Optional):
- For a creamier texture, you can use an immersion blender to partially blend the soup. This step is optional, and you can leave the soup chunky if you prefer.

Add Truffle Oil:
- Stir in the truffle oil, adjusting the amount to your taste. Truffle oil is potent, so start with a small amount and add more if needed.

Serve:
- Ladle the White Bean and Truffle Oil Soup into bowls.

Garnish (Optional):
- Garnish with fresh parsley and serve with grated Parmesan cheese on the side if desired.

Enjoy:
- Enjoy this flavorful and sophisticated White Bean and Truffle Oil Soup as a comforting and gourmet appetizer or main course!

The truffle oil adds a luxurious touch to the creamy white bean soup, creating a dish that's both comforting and indulgent. It's perfect for a special meal or when you want to elevate your soup experience.

Salads

Watercress, Blood Orange, and Pomegranate Salad

Ingredients:

For the Salad:

- 1 bunch watercress, tough stems removed
- 2 blood oranges, peeled and segmented
- 1/2 cup pomegranate seeds
- 1/4 cup crumbled feta cheese (optional)
- 1/4 cup toasted walnuts or almonds, chopped

For the Dressing:

- 2 tablespoons extra-virgin olive oil
- 1 tablespoon balsamic vinegar
- 1 teaspoon honey
- Salt and black pepper to taste

Instructions:

Prepare Watercress:

- Wash and thoroughly dry the watercress. Remove any tough stems and place the tender leaves in a large salad bowl.

Peel and Segment Blood Oranges:

- Peel the blood oranges and carefully segment them, removing any pith. If you prefer, you can also slice the oranges into rounds.

Assemble Salad:

- Add the blood orange segments to the salad bowl with watercress. Sprinkle pomegranate seeds over the top.

Optional Feta Cheese:

- If using feta cheese, crumble it over the salad.

Add Toasted Nuts:

- Sprinkle the chopped toasted walnuts or almonds on top.

Make Dressing:

- In a small bowl, whisk together extra-virgin olive oil, balsamic vinegar, honey, salt, and black pepper to create the dressing.

Drizzle Dressing:

- Drizzle the dressing over the salad just before serving. Toss gently to coat the ingredients evenly.

Serve:

- Transfer the Watercress, Blood Orange, and Pomegranate Salad to a serving platter or individual plates.

Enjoy:

- Enjoy this refreshing and colorful salad as a side dish or a light and healthy main course!

This salad offers a delightful combination of textures and flavors, with the crispness of watercress, the juiciness of blood oranges, the burst of sweetness from pomegranate seeds, and the savory notes of feta cheese. It's a perfect addition to your menu for a light and vibrant meal.

Pear, Gouda, and Candied Pecan Salad with White Balsamic Vinaigrette

Ingredients:

For the Salad:

- 4 cups mixed salad greens (arugula, spinach, or your choice)
- 2 ripe pears, thinly sliced
- 1 cup Gouda cheese, shaved or diced
- 1/2 cup candied pecans, roughly chopped

For the White Balsamic Vinaigrette:

- 1/4 cup white balsamic vinegar
- 1/2 cup extra-virgin olive oil
- 1 tablespoon Dijon mustard
- 1 teaspoon honey
- Salt and black pepper to taste

Instructions:

Prepare Salad Greens:

- Wash and dry the mixed salad greens. Place them in a large salad bowl.

Slice Pears:

- Thinly slice the ripe pears and arrange them on top of the salad greens.

Add Gouda Cheese:

- Shave or dice Gouda cheese and scatter it over the salad.

Sprinkle Candied Pecans:

- Sprinkle the roughly chopped candied pecans over the salad for a delightful crunch.

Make White Balsamic Vinaigrette:

- In a small bowl, whisk together white balsamic vinegar, extra-virgin olive oil, Dijon mustard, honey, salt, and black pepper. Adjust the seasoning to your taste.

Drizzle Dressing:

- Drizzle the white balsamic vinaigrette over the salad just before serving.

Toss Gently:

- Toss the salad gently to coat the ingredients evenly with the vinaigrette.

Serve:

- Transfer the Pear, Gouda, and Candied Pecan Salad to a serving platter or individual plates.

Enjoy:

- Enjoy this flavorful and sophisticated salad as a refreshing side dish or a light and healthy main course!

The combination of sweet pears, creamy Gouda, crunchy candied pecans, and tangy vinaigrette creates a well-balanced and delicious salad that's perfect for special occasions or a delightful everyday meal.

Main Courses - Seafood

Seared Scallops with Lemon Beurre Blanc

Ingredients:

For the Scallops:

- 12 large sea scallops, patted dry
- Salt and black pepper to taste
- 2 tablespoons olive oil
- 1 tablespoon unsalted butter

For the Lemon Beurre Blanc:

- 1/2 cup dry white wine
- 1/4 cup white wine vinegar
- 1 shallot, finely chopped
- 1 tablespoon fresh lemon juice
- 1/2 cup unsalted butter, cold and cut into cubes
- Salt and white pepper to taste
- Lemon zest for garnish (optional)
- Fresh parsley for garnish (optional)

Instructions:

Prepare Scallops:

- Pat the scallops dry with paper towels. Season both sides with salt and black pepper.

Sear Scallops:

- In a large skillet, heat olive oil and 1 tablespoon of butter over medium-high heat. Once hot, add the scallops to the skillet, making sure not to overcrowd them. Sear for 2-3 minutes on each side or until golden brown and cooked through. Remove the scallops from the skillet and set them aside.

Make Lemon Beurre Blanc:

- In the same skillet, add white wine, white wine vinegar, and chopped shallot. Bring the mixture to a simmer and cook until it's reduced by half.

Add Lemon Juice:

- Stir in fresh lemon juice and continue to simmer for another minute.

Incorporate Butter:

- Reduce the heat to low. Begin adding the cold butter cubes to the sauce, one or two at a time, whisking continuously. Continue this process until all the butter is incorporated and the sauce is smooth.

Season and Garnish:

- Season the lemon beurre blanc with salt and white pepper to taste. If desired, add lemon zest for extra citrus flavor.

Plate:

- Arrange the seared scallops on serving plates.

Sauce Scallops:

- Spoon the lemon beurre blanc sauce over the scallops.

Garnish (Optional):

- Garnish with fresh parsley and additional lemon zest if desired.

Serve:

- Serve the Seared Scallops with Lemon Beurre Blanc immediately while the scallops are still hot and the sauce is velvety.

Enjoy:

- Enjoy this restaurant-quality dish with the perfect balance of seared scallops and a luscious lemon butter sauce!

This dish is perfect for a special occasion or a romantic dinner. The combination of the sweet, tender scallops and the silky lemon beurre blanc creates a delightful culinary experience.

Pan-Roasted Halibut with Saffron Cream Sauce

Ingredients:

For the Halibut:

- 4 halibut fillets (6-8 ounces each), skin removed
- Salt and black pepper to taste
- 2 tablespoons olive oil
- 1 tablespoon unsalted butter

For the Saffron Cream Sauce:

- 1/2 cup dry white wine
- 1/4 teaspoon saffron threads
- 1 cup heavy cream
- 2 tablespoons unsalted butter
- Salt and white pepper to taste
- Fresh chives for garnish (optional)
- Lemon wedges for serving

Instructions:

Prepare Halibut:

- Pat the halibut fillets dry with paper towels. Season both sides with salt and black pepper.

Infuse Saffron:

- In a small bowl, combine the dry white wine and saffron threads. Let them steep for about 10-15 minutes to infuse the saffron flavor into the wine.

Sear Halibut:

- In a large skillet, heat olive oil and 1 tablespoon of butter over medium-high heat. Once hot, add the halibut fillets to the skillet. Sear for 3-4 minutes on each side or until the fish is golden brown and cooked through. Transfer the halibut to a plate and cover with foil to keep warm.

Make Saffron Cream Sauce:

- In the same skillet, add the saffron-infused white wine and bring it to a simmer. Scrape any browned bits from the bottom of the skillet.

Add Cream:

- Pour in the heavy cream and simmer for 2-3 minutes, allowing the sauce to thicken slightly.

Incorporate Butter:

- Stir in 2 tablespoons of unsalted butter to the sauce, allowing it to melt and create a rich, velvety texture.

Season:

- Season the saffron cream sauce with salt and white pepper to taste. Adjust the seasoning if needed.

Plate:

- Place the pan-roasted halibut fillets on serving plates.

Sauce Halibut:

- Spoon the saffron cream sauce over the halibut fillets.

Garnish (Optional):

- Garnish with fresh chives for a burst of color and additional flavor.

Serve:

- Serve the Pan-Roasted Halibut with Saffron Cream Sauce immediately with lemon wedges on the side.

Enjoy:

- Enjoy this decadent and sophisticated dish, savoring the combination of perfectly seared halibut and the aromatic saffron cream sauce!

This dish is perfect for a special dinner and pairs wonderfully with a side of steamed vegetables or a bed of saffron-infused rice.

Lobster Risotto with Truffle Oil

Ingredients:

- 1 1/2 cups Arborio rice
- 1/2 cup dry white wine
- 1 shallot, finely chopped
- 2 tablespoons olive oil
- 2 tablespoons unsalted butter
- 1 pound lobster meat, cooked and chopped
- 4 cups seafood or chicken broth, kept warm
- 1/2 cup grated Parmesan cheese
- Salt and black pepper to taste
- 1 tablespoon truffle oil
- Fresh chives for garnish (optional)
- Lemon wedges for serving

Instructions:

Prepare Lobster:

- Cook the lobster meat using your preferred method (boiling, steaming, or grilling).

    Once cooked, chop the lobster into bite-sized pieces.

Sauté Shallot:

- In a large skillet or saucepan, heat olive oil over medium heat. Add the finely chopped shallot and sauté until softened.

Toast Rice:

- Add Arborio rice to the skillet and cook for 1-2 minutes, stirring frequently, until the rice is lightly toasted.

Deglaze with Wine:

- Pour in the white wine to deglaze the skillet, scraping any browned bits from the bottom.

Add Broth:

- Begin adding the warm seafood or chicken broth, one ladle at a time. Allow the liquid to be absorbed by the rice before adding the next ladle. Continue stirring frequently.

Cook Risotto:

- Continue this process until the rice is creamy and cooked to al dente, usually around 18-20 minutes.

Incorporate Lobster:

- Stir in the chopped lobster meat during the last 5 minutes of cooking, allowing it to heat through and infuse the risotto with its flavor.

Finish with Butter and Cheese:

- Once the rice is cooked, stir in unsalted butter and grated Parmesan cheese. Season with salt and black pepper to taste.

Drizzle Truffle Oil:

- Drizzle truffle oil over the risotto and stir to incorporate, giving the dish its distinctive aroma.

Garnish (Optional):

- Garnish with fresh chives for a burst of color and additional flavor.

Serve:

- Serve the Lobster Risotto with Truffle Oil hot, accompanied by lemon wedges on the side.

Enjoy:

- Enjoy this decadent Lobster Risotto as a centerpiece for a special occasion or a delightful gourmet meal!

This dish brings together the richness of lobster, the creamy texture of risotto, and the luxurious aroma of truffle oil for a truly special dining experience.

Citrus and Herb Grilled Shrimp Skewers

Ingredients:

For the Marinade:

- 1/4 cup olive oil
- 2 tablespoons fresh orange juice
- 2 tablespoons fresh lemon juice
- 1 tablespoon fresh lime juice
- 2 cloves garlic, minced
- 1 teaspoon honey or maple syrup
- 1 teaspoon fresh thyme, chopped
- 1 teaspoon fresh rosemary, chopped
- Salt and black pepper to taste

For the Shrimp:

- 1 pound large shrimp, peeled and deveined
- Wooden or metal skewers (if using wooden, soak them in water for 30 minutes)

For Garnish (Optional):

- Fresh herbs (thyme, rosemary, or cilantro)
- Lemon and orange wedges

Instructions:

    Prepare Marinade:

- In a bowl, whisk together olive oil, fresh orange juice, fresh lemon juice, fresh lime juice, minced garlic, honey or maple syrup, chopped thyme, chopped rosemary, salt, and black pepper.

Marinate Shrimp:

- Place the peeled and deveined shrimp in a shallow dish or a large zip-top bag. Pour the marinade over the shrimp, ensuring they are well-coated. Marinate in the refrigerator for at least 30 minutes to allow the flavors to infuse.

Preheat Grill:

- Preheat your grill to medium-high heat.

Skewer Shrimp:

- Thread the marinated shrimp onto the skewers, leaving space between each shrimp.

Grill Shrimp:

- Grill the shrimp skewers for 2-3 minutes per side or until they are opaque and have grill marks.

Baste with Marinade:

- While grilling, baste the shrimp with some of the reserved marinade to enhance the flavors.

Garnish (Optional):

- Garnish the grilled shrimp skewers with fresh herbs such as thyme, rosemary, or cilantro. Serve with lemon and orange wedges on the side.

Serve:

- Arrange the Citrus and Herb Grilled Shrimp Skewers on a platter and serve hot.

Enjoy:

- Enjoy these flavorful shrimp skewers as a delicious appetizer or main course. They pair well with rice, quinoa, or a fresh salad.

The combination of citrus and herbs creates a bright and zesty flavor profile, making these grilled shrimp skewers a perfect addition to your outdoor dining or barbecue experience.

Salmon en Papillote with Dill and Lemon

Ingredients:

- 4 salmon fillets
- Salt and black pepper to taste
- 2 tablespoons olive oil
- 4 slices of lemon
- 4 sprigs fresh dill
- 1 small red onion, thinly sliced
- 1 zucchini, thinly sliced
- 1 carrot, thinly sliced
- Parchment paper

Instructions:

Preheat Oven:

- Preheat your oven to 400°F (200°C).

Prepare Parchment Paper:

- Cut four large squares of parchment paper, each large enough to wrap around a salmon fillet.

Season Salmon:

- Place a salmon fillet in the center of each parchment paper square. Season with salt and black pepper.

Add Vegetables:

- Arrange slices of lemon, sprigs of fresh dill, red onion, zucchini, and carrot on top of each salmon fillet.

Drizzle with Olive Oil:

- Drizzle each salmon fillet with olive oil.

Seal Parchment Packets:

- Fold the parchment paper over the salmon and vegetables, then seal the edges by folding and crimping to create a sealed packet.

Bake in Oven:

- Place the sealed parchment packets on a baking sheet and bake in the preheated oven for 15-20 minutes or until the salmon is cooked through.

Serve:

- Carefully open the parchment paper packets at the table to release the aromatic steam. Serve the Salmon en Papillote directly from the parchment.

Enjoy:

- Enjoy this delicious and healthy Salmon en Papillote with Dill and Lemon!

This cooking method allows the salmon to cook in its juices, along with the infused flavors of dill, lemon, and vegetables. It's a visually impressive and flavorful dish that's easy to prepare for a quick and elegant meal.

Miso-Glazed Black Cod with Sesame Ginger Broccolini

Ingredients:

For the Miso-Glazed Black Cod:

- 4 black cod fillets (about 6 ounces each), skin-on
- 1/4 cup white miso paste
- 2 tablespoons mirin
- 2 tablespoons sake (or dry white wine)
- 2 tablespoons maple syrup or honey
- 1 tablespoon soy sauce
- 1 tablespoon rice vinegar
- 1 teaspoon grated fresh ginger
- Sesame seeds for garnish (optional)
- Sliced green onions for garnish (optional)

For the Sesame Ginger Broccolini:

- 1 bunch broccolini, trimmed
- 1 tablespoon sesame oil
- 1 tablespoon soy sauce
- 1 tablespoon rice vinegar
- 1 teaspoon grated fresh ginger
- Sesame seeds for garnish (optional)

Instructions:

Preheat Oven:

- Preheat your oven to 400°F (200°C).

Prepare Miso Glaze:
- In a bowl, whisk together white miso paste, mirin, sake, maple syrup or honey, soy sauce, rice vinegar, and grated fresh ginger to create the miso glaze.

Marinate Black Cod:
- Place the black cod fillets in a shallow dish and brush them generously with the miso glaze, ensuring all sides are coated. Let them marinate for at least 30 minutes in the refrigerator.

Bake Black Cod:
- Place the marinated black cod fillets on a baking sheet lined with parchment paper. Bake in the preheated oven for 12-15 minutes or until the fish is opaque and flakes easily.

Prepare Sesame Ginger Broccolini:
- While the black cod is baking, steam or blanch the broccolini until crisp-tender. In a separate bowl, whisk together sesame oil, soy sauce, rice vinegar, and grated fresh ginger.

Sauté Broccolini:
- In a pan, heat the sesame oil mixture over medium-high heat. Add the steamed broccolini and sauté for 2-3 minutes until well-coated and heated through.

Serve:
- Plate the Miso-Glazed Black Cod on individual plates, top with sesame seeds and sliced green onions if desired. Serve alongside the Sesame Ginger Broccolini.

Garnish (Optional):

- Garnish the dish with additional sesame seeds and sliced green onions if desired.

Enjoy:

- Enjoy this exquisite Miso-Glazed Black Cod with Sesame Ginger Broccolini as a restaurant-worthy meal right at home!

The combination of the sweet and savory miso glaze on the black cod, paired with the sesame ginger broccolini, creates a harmonious and delicious dining experience.

Cioppino (Italian Seafood Stew) with Garlic Bread

Ingredients:

For the Seafood Broth:

- 2 tablespoons olive oil
- 1 onion, finely chopped
- 2 celery stalks, finely chopped
- 1 fennel bulb, thinly sliced
- 4 garlic cloves, minced
- 1 teaspoon dried oregano
- 1 teaspoon dried basil
- 1/2 teaspoon red pepper flakes (adjust to taste)
- 1 bay leaf
- 1 cup white wine
- 1 (28 oz) can crushed tomatoes
- 1 (14 oz) can diced tomatoes
- 4 cups fish or seafood broth
- Salt and black pepper to taste

For the Seafood:

- 1 pound mussels, cleaned and debearded
- 1 pound clams, cleaned
- 1/2 pound large shrimp, peeled and deveined
- 1/2 pound firm white fish fillets, cut into chunks (such as cod or halibut)
- 1/2 pound calamari rings
- 1/2 pound crab legs or crab claws (optional)

For the Garlic Bread:

- 1 French baguette, sliced
- 1/2 cup unsalted butter, softened
- 4 garlic cloves, minced
- 2 tablespoons fresh parsley, chopped
- Salt to taste

Instructions:

For the Seafood Broth:

In a large pot or Dutch oven, heat olive oil over medium heat. Add chopped onion, celery, and sliced fennel. Cook until vegetables are softened, about 5 minutes. Add minced garlic, dried oregano, dried basil, red pepper flakes, and bay leaf. Cook for an additional 2 minutes until fragrant.
Pour in white wine, scraping any browned bits from the bottom of the pot. Allow the wine to reduce by half.
Add crushed tomatoes, diced tomatoes, fish or seafood broth, salt, and black pepper. Bring the mixture to a simmer, then reduce heat to low and let it simmer for 20-30 minutes to allow the flavors to meld.

For the Seafood:

Add the seafood to the simmering broth. Start with the clams and mussels, as they take longer to cook. Once they begin to open, add shrimp, calamari, and chunks of fish. If using crab legs, add them at this point as well.
Cook until all the seafood is fully cooked and the mussels and clams have opened. Discard any unopened shells.

For the Garlic Bread:

Preheat the oven to broil.
In a small bowl, mix softened butter, minced garlic, chopped parsley, and a pinch of salt.
Spread the garlic butter mixture on the sliced baguette.
Place the garlic bread slices on a baking sheet and broil for 1-2 minutes or until golden and slightly crispy.

Serve:

Ladle the Cioppino into bowls, making sure to include a variety of seafood in each serving.
Serve the garlic bread on the side for dipping into the delicious broth.
Garnish with additional chopped parsley if desired.
Enjoy this delightful Cioppino with Garlic Bread as a comforting and flavorful seafood feast!

Main Courses - Meat:

Filet Mignon with Red Wine Reduction

Ingredients:

For the Filet Mignon:

- 4 filet mignon steaks (about 6-8 ounces each)
- Salt and black pepper to taste
- 2 tablespoons olive oil
- 2 cloves garlic, minced
- 2 sprigs fresh rosemary or thyme

For the Red Wine Reduction Sauce:

- 1 cup red wine (choose a good quality wine)
- 1/2 cup beef broth
- 1 shallot, finely chopped
- 2 tablespoons unsalted butter
- Salt and black pepper to taste

Instructions:

For the Filet Mignon:

Preheat Oven:
- Preheat your oven to 400°F (200°C).

Season Steaks:

- Pat the filet mignon steaks dry with paper towels. Season generously with salt and black pepper on both sides.

Sear Steaks:

- In an oven-safe skillet, heat olive oil over medium-high heat. Add the filet mignon steaks and sear on each side for 2-3 minutes or until a golden crust forms.

Add Aromatics:

- Add minced garlic and fresh rosemary or thyme sprigs to the skillet. Transfer the skillet to the preheated oven.

Roast in Oven:

- Roast the filet mignon in the oven for 5-7 minutes for medium-rare, or longer if you prefer a different level of doneness.

Rest Steaks:

- Remove the skillet from the oven and transfer the steaks to a plate. Let them rest for a few minutes while you prepare the red wine reduction.

For the Red Wine Reduction Sauce:

Deglaze Skillet:

- Place the skillet back on the stovetop over medium heat. Add chopped shallot and sauté until softened. Deglaze the skillet with red wine, scraping up any browned bits from the bottom.

Reduce Wine:

- Allow the red wine to reduce by half, then add beef broth and continue simmering.

Finish Sauce:

- Whisk in unsalted butter to finish the sauce. Season with salt and black pepper to taste.

Strain (Optional):

- For a smoother sauce, you can strain out the shallot and any herb remnants.

Serve:

Plate Steaks:

- Place the rested filet mignon steaks on serving plates.

Pour Sauce:

- Pour the red wine reduction sauce over each steak.

Garnish (Optional):

- Garnish with additional fresh herbs if desired.

Enjoy:

- Enjoy this Filet Mignon with Red Wine Reduction as a decadent and luxurious meal!

Serve with your favorite side dishes such as mashed potatoes or roasted vegetables to complete the dining experience.

Duck Confit with Orange Gastrique

Ingredients:

For the Duck Confit:

- 4 duck leg quarters
- 4 cups duck fat (or a combination of duck fat and olive oil)
- 4 cloves garlic, crushed
- 4 sprigs fresh thyme
- Salt and black pepper to taste

For the Orange Gastrique:

- 1 cup orange juice (freshly squeezed is preferable)
- 1/2 cup red wine vinegar
- 1/4 cup honey
- 1 tablespoon Dijon mustard
- Salt and black pepper to taste

Instructions:

For the Duck Confit:

Preheat Oven:
- Preheat your oven to 325°F (163°C).

Season Duck Legs:
- Season the duck leg quarters with salt and black pepper on both sides.

Place in Baking Dish:

- Place the duck leg quarters in a baking dish or oven-safe skillet. Add crushed garlic and fresh thyme sprigs around and on top of the duck.

Submerge in Duck Fat:

- Pour the duck fat (or duck fat and olive oil mixture) over the duck legs, ensuring they are fully submerged.

Bake:

- Cover the baking dish with foil and bake in the preheated oven for 2.5 to 3 hours or until the duck is tender and easily pulls away from the bone.

Crisp the Skin (Optional):

- For crispier skin, you can pan-sear the duck legs in a hot skillet for a few minutes before serving.

For the Orange Gastrique:

Prepare Gastrique:

- In a saucepan, combine orange juice, red wine vinegar, honey, and Dijon mustard. Bring to a simmer over medium heat.

Reduce Sauce:

- Allow the mixture to simmer and reduce until it thickens to a syrupy consistency.

Season:

- Season the orange gastrique with salt and black pepper to taste.

Serve:

Plate Duck Confit:

- Place the duck confit on serving plates.

Drizzle with Gastrique:

- Drizzle the orange gastrique over the duck confit.

Garnish (Optional):

- Garnish with fresh thyme leaves or orange zest if desired.

Enjoy:

- Enjoy this Duck Confit with Orange Gastrique as a luxurious and flavorful main course!

Serve the duck confit with a side of roasted vegetables, mashed potatoes, or a simple salad to complement the richness of the dish.

Herb-Crusted Rack of Lamb with Mint Pesto

Ingredients:

For the Herb-Crusted Rack of Lamb:

- 2 racks of lamb, frenched (about 8 ribs each)
- Salt and black pepper to taste
- 2 tablespoons Dijon mustard
- 2 tablespoons olive oil
- 3 cloves garlic, minced
- 1 tablespoon fresh rosemary, chopped
- 1 tablespoon fresh thyme, chopped
- 1 cup breadcrumbs (preferably Panko)

For the Mint Pesto:

- 1 cup fresh mint leaves, packed
- 1/2 cup fresh parsley leaves, packed
- 1/4 cup pine nuts, toasted
- 1/2 cup grated Parmesan cheese
- 2 cloves garlic, peeled
- 1/2 cup extra-virgin olive oil
- Salt and black pepper to taste
- Juice of 1 lemon

Instructions:

For the Herb-Crusted Rack of Lamb:

Preheat Oven:

- Preheat your oven to 400°F (200°C).

Season Lamb:

- Season the racks of lamb with salt and black pepper. Place them on a plate.

Mix Mustard and Herbs:

- In a small bowl, mix Dijon mustard, olive oil, minced garlic, chopped rosemary, and chopped thyme.

Coat Lamb with Mustard Mixture:

- Brush the racks of lamb with the mustard mixture, ensuring they are well coated.

Coat with Breadcrumbs:

- Press breadcrumbs onto the mustard-coated lamb to create a crust.

Sear in Pan (Optional):

- If desired, you can sear the racks of lamb in a hot skillet for a couple of minutes on each side to develop a golden crust before roasting.

Roast in Oven:

- Place the racks of lamb on a roasting pan and roast in the preheated oven for 20-25 minutes for medium-rare or longer if you prefer a different level of doneness.

Rest:

- Allow the lamb to rest for a few minutes before slicing.

For the Mint Pesto:

Toast Pine Nuts:

- In a dry skillet, toast the pine nuts over medium heat until golden brown. Be careful not to burn them.

Prepare Pesto:

- In a food processor, combine mint leaves, parsley leaves, toasted pine nuts, grated Parmesan cheese, peeled garlic cloves, and lemon juice. Pulse until coarsely chopped.

Stream in Olive Oil:

- With the food processor running, slowly stream in the extra-virgin olive oil until the pesto reaches your desired consistency.

Season:

- Season the mint pesto with salt and black pepper to taste. Adjust the lemon juice if needed.

Serve:

Slice Lamb:

- Slice the herb-crusted rack of lamb into individual chops.

Drizzle with Pesto:

- Drizzle the mint pesto over the sliced lamb or serve it on the side.

Garnish (Optional):

- Garnish with additional fresh mint leaves or a sprinkle of Parmesan if desired.

Enjoy:

- Enjoy this Herb-Crusted Rack of Lamb with Mint Pesto as a stunning and flavorful main course!

Serve with your favorite sides, such as roasted vegetables, mashed potatoes, or a fresh salad.

Coq au Vin

Ingredients:

- 1 whole chicken (about 3-4 pounds), cut into pieces
- Salt and black pepper to taste
- 4 tablespoons all-purpose flour
- 4 tablespoons olive oil
- 8 ounces bacon, diced
- 1 onion, finely chopped
- 2 carrots, sliced
- 3 cloves garlic, minced
- 1 tablespoon tomato paste
- 2 cups red wine (preferably a Burgundy or other dry red wine)
- 2 cups chicken broth
- 2 bay leaves
- 1 teaspoon dried thyme
- 1 pound mushrooms, quartered
- 2 tablespoons butter
- Chopped fresh parsley for garnish

Instructions:

Preheat Oven:

- Preheat your oven to 350°F (175°C).

Season Chicken:

- Season the chicken pieces with salt and black pepper. Dredge the chicken in flour, shaking off any excess.

Brown Chicken:

- In a large Dutch oven or oven-safe pot, heat olive oil over medium-high heat. Brown the chicken pieces on all sides. Work in batches to avoid overcrowding the pot. Remove the browned chicken and set aside.

Sauté Bacon and Vegetables:

- In the same pot, add diced bacon and cook until crispy. Add chopped onion, sliced carrots, and minced garlic. Sauté until the vegetables are softened.

Add Tomato Paste:

- Stir in the tomato paste and cook for 1-2 minutes.

Deglaze with Wine:

- Pour in the red wine to deglaze the pot, scraping up any browned bits from the bottom.

Add Chicken, Broth, and Herbs:

- Return the browned chicken to the pot. Add chicken broth, bay leaves, and dried thyme. Bring to a simmer.

Braise in Oven:

- Cover the pot and transfer it to the preheated oven. Braise for 45 minutes to 1 hour or until the chicken is tender.

Sauté Mushrooms:

- In a separate skillet, melt butter and sauté quartered mushrooms until they are browned and cooked through.

Add Mushrooms:

- Add the sautéed mushrooms to the pot, stirring gently.

Adjust Seasoning:

- Taste and adjust the seasoning with salt and black pepper if needed.

Serve:

- Remove bay leaves and serve Coq au Vin hot, garnished with chopped fresh parsley.

Enjoy:

- Enjoy this classic Coq au Vin with crusty bread, mashed potatoes, or over egg noodles.

Coq au Vin is a wonderful dish that brings together rich flavors from the wine, tender chicken, and aromatic herbs. It's a delightful and satisfying meal that pairs well with a glass of red wine.

Coffee-Rubbed Lamb Chops with Rosemary Demi-Glace

Ingredients:

For the Coffee Rub:

- 2 tablespoons ground coffee
- 1 tablespoon brown sugar
- 1 teaspoon smoked paprika
- 1 teaspoon garlic powder
- 1 teaspoon onion powder
- 1 teaspoon salt
- 1/2 teaspoon black pepper
- 1/2 teaspoon dried thyme

For the Lamb Chops:

- 4 lamb chops (about 1 inch thick)
- Olive oil for searing

For the Rosemary Demi-Glace:

- 1 cup beef or lamb broth
- 1/2 cup red wine
- 1 tablespoon balsamic vinegar
- 2 sprigs fresh rosemary
- 1 tablespoon unsalted butter
- Salt and black pepper to taste

Instructions:

For the Coffee Rub:

Mix Ingredients:

- In a small bowl, combine ground coffee, brown sugar, smoked paprika, garlic powder, onion powder, salt, black pepper, and dried thyme. Mix well to create the coffee rub.

For the Lamb Chops:

Preheat Oven:

- Preheat your oven to 400°F (200°C).

Season Lamb Chops:

- Pat the lamb chops dry with paper towels. Rub the coffee rub generously on both sides of each lamb chop.

Sear Lamb Chops:

- In an oven-safe skillet, heat olive oil over medium-high heat. Sear the lamb chops for 2-3 minutes on each side or until a golden crust forms.

Transfer to Oven:

- Transfer the skillet to the preheated oven and roast for 10-15 minutes or until the lamb reaches your desired level of doneness.

Rest Lamb Chops:

- Remove the lamb chops from the oven and let them rest for a few minutes before serving.

For the Rosemary Demi-Glace:

Prepare Demi-Glace:

- In a saucepan, combine beef or lamb broth, red wine, balsamic vinegar, and fresh rosemary sprigs. Simmer over medium heat until the liquid is reduced by half.

Strain and Finish Sauce:

- Strain the liquid to remove rosemary and any solids. Return the strained liquid to the saucepan, add unsalted butter, and continue simmering until the sauce thickens slightly. Season with salt and black pepper to taste.

Serve:

Plate Lamb Chops:

- Arrange the coffee-rubbed lamb chops on serving plates.

Drizzle with Demi-Glace:

- Drizzle the rosemary demi-glace over the lamb chops.

Garnish (Optional):

- Garnish with fresh rosemary leaves for an extra touch.

Enjoy:

- Enjoy these Coffee-Rubbed Lamb Chops with Rosemary Demi-Glace for a unique and flavorful dining experience!

Serve the lamb chops with your favorite side dishes, such as mashed potatoes or roasted vegetables, to complement the robust flavors of the coffee rub and the rich demi-glace.

Dijon and Herb-Crusted Pork Tenderloin with Apple Compote

Ingredients:

For the Pork Tenderloin:

- 2 pork tenderloins (about 1.5 pounds each)
- Salt and black pepper to taste
- 2 tablespoons Dijon mustard
- 2 tablespoons whole-grain mustard
- 2 tablespoons olive oil
- 2 cloves garlic, minced
- 1 tablespoon fresh rosemary, chopped
- 1 tablespoon fresh thyme, chopped
- 1 cup breadcrumbs (panko or regular)

For the Apple Compote:

- 3 apples, peeled, cored, and diced (use a variety like Granny Smith for a balance of sweetness and tartness)
- 2 tablespoons unsalted butter
- 2 tablespoons brown sugar
- 1 teaspoon ground cinnamon
- 1/4 cup apple cider or apple juice
- 1 tablespoon lemon juice

Instructions:

For the Pork Tenderloin:

Preheat Oven:
- Preheat your oven to 400°F (200°C).

Season Pork:
- Season the pork tenderloins with salt and black pepper.

Mix Mustard and Herbs:
- In a bowl, combine Dijon mustard, whole-grain mustard, olive oil, minced garlic, chopped rosemary, and chopped thyme.

Coat with Mustard Mixture:
- Coat the pork tenderloins with the mustard mixture, ensuring they are well covered.

Crust with Breadcrumbs:
- Press breadcrumbs onto the mustard-coated pork to create a crust.

Sear in Pan (Optional):
- If desired, you can sear the pork tenderloins in a hot oven-safe skillet for a couple of minutes on each side to develop a golden crust before roasting.

Roast in Oven:
- Place the pork tenderloins on a baking sheet or in the skillet if searing, and roast in the preheated oven for 20-25 minutes or until the internal temperature reaches 145°F (63°C).

Rest:
- Allow the pork to rest for a few minutes before slicing.

For the Apple Compote:

Cook Apples:

- In a saucepan, melt unsalted butter over medium heat. Add diced apples, brown sugar, ground cinnamon, apple cider (or apple juice), and lemon juice.

Simmer:

- Simmer the mixture until the apples are tender and the liquid has reduced, creating a compote-like consistency. This should take about 10-12 minutes.

Adjust Sweetness:

- Adjust the sweetness by adding more brown sugar if needed.

Serve:

Slice Pork:

- Slice the Dijon and herb-crusted pork tenderloin into medallions.

Plate with Apple Compote:

- Arrange the pork slices on serving plates and spoon the apple compote over the top.

Garnish (Optional):

- Garnish with additional fresh herbs for a decorative touch.

Enjoy:

- Enjoy this Dijon and Herb-Crusted Pork Tenderloin with Apple Compote as a delicious and well-balanced meal!

Serve with your favorite sides, such as roasted vegetables, mashed potatoes, or a green salad. The combination of savory and sweet flavors makes this dish a crowd-pleaser.

Veal Saltimbocca with Sage and Prosciutto

Ingredients:

For the Veal:

- 4 veal cutlets, pounded to an even thickness
- Salt and black pepper to taste
- 8 fresh sage leaves
- 4 slices prosciutto
- All-purpose flour for dredging
- 2 tablespoons olive oil
- 2 tablespoons unsalted butter

For the Pan Sauce:

- 1/2 cup dry white wine
- 1/2 cup chicken or veal broth
- 2 tablespoons fresh lemon juice
- 2 tablespoons capers, drained
- 2 tablespoons unsalted butter

Instructions:

For the Veal:

Season Veal:
- Season the veal cutlets with salt and black pepper.

Add Sage and Prosciutto:

- Place a sage leaf on each veal cutlet and wrap with a slice of prosciutto, securing it with a toothpick.

Dredge in Flour:

- Dredge each veal cutlet in flour, shaking off any excess.

Sear in Pan:

- In a large skillet, heat olive oil and 2 tablespoons of butter over medium-high heat. Add the veal cutlets and cook for 2-3 minutes on each side or until the prosciutto is crisp, and the veal is cooked to your desired level of doneness.

Remove Toothpicks:

- Remove the toothpicks from the veal and transfer the cutlets to a plate. Cover to keep warm.

For the Pan Sauce:

Deglaze Pan:

- Pour the white wine into the skillet, scraping up any browned bits from the bottom. Allow it to simmer for a minute.

Add Broth, Lemon Juice, and Capers:

- Add chicken or veal broth, fresh lemon juice, and capers to the skillet. Simmer for another 2-3 minutes.

Finish with Butter:

- Stir in 2 tablespoons of unsalted butter to finish the sauce. Adjust the seasoning with salt and pepper if needed.

Serve:

Plate Veal:

- Place the veal saltimbocca on serving plates.

Drizzle with Pan Sauce:

- Spoon the pan sauce over the veal.

Garnish (Optional):

- Garnish with additional fresh sage leaves or a sprinkle of chopped parsley.

Enjoy:

- Enjoy this Veal Saltimbocca with Sage and Prosciutto with your favorite side dishes, such as risotto or mashed potatoes!

The combination of tender veal, aromatic sage, and the salty kick from prosciutto makes this dish a delightful experience. The pan sauce adds a burst of flavor that complements the richness of the veal.

Pasta and Risotto

Lobster and Champagne Risotto

Ingredients:

- 1 1/2 cups Arborio rice
- 1/2 cup dry white wine (Champagne or sparkling wine)
- 4 cups seafood or chicken broth, kept warm
- 1 cup cooked lobster meat, chopped into bite-sized pieces
- 1/2 cup grated Parmesan cheese
- 1/4 cup heavy cream
- 1/4 cup shallots, finely chopped
- 2 cloves garlic, minced
- 1/2 cup dry Champagne or sparkling wine
- 2 tablespoons olive oil
- 2 tablespoons unsalted butter
- Salt and black pepper to taste
- Chopped fresh parsley for garnish

Instructions:

Prepare Lobster:

- If you haven't cooked the lobster yet, steam or boil it until fully cooked. Remove the meat from the shell and chop it into bite-sized pieces.

Heat Broth:

- In a saucepan, heat the seafood or chicken broth over low heat to keep it warm.

Sauté Shallots and Garlic:

- In a large, deep skillet or Dutch oven, heat olive oil and 1 tablespoon of butter over medium heat. Add finely chopped shallots and minced garlic. Sauté until they are softened.

Toast Arborio Rice:

- Add Arborio rice to the skillet and cook, stirring, for 1-2 minutes until the rice is lightly toasted.

Deglaze with Wine:

- Pour 1/2 cup of dry white wine (Champagne or sparkling wine) into the skillet, stirring constantly until the wine is mostly absorbed.

Add Broth:

- Begin adding the warm broth, one ladle at a time, stirring frequently. Allow the liquid to be mostly absorbed before adding the next ladle of broth. Continue this process until the rice is creamy and cooked to al dente texture. This should take about 18-20 minutes.

Incorporate Lobster:

- About halfway through the cooking process, add the chopped lobster meat to the risotto, allowing it to infuse with the flavors.

Finish Risotto:

- Once the rice is cooked, stir in the remaining tablespoon of butter, heavy cream, and grated Parmesan cheese. Season with salt and black pepper to taste.

Finish with Champagne:

- Just before serving, pour 1/2 cup of dry Champagne or sparkling wine into the risotto and stir gently. This adds a touch of effervescence to the dish.

Garnish and Serve:

- Garnish the Lobster and Champagne Risotto with chopped fresh parsley. Serve immediately.

Enjoy:

- Enjoy this decadent Lobster and Champagne Risotto as a luxurious main course for a special occasion or celebration!

Pair the risotto with a glass of Champagne to complement the flavors and elevate the dining experience. Serve it with a side of crusty bread or a light salad for a well-rounded meal.

Truffle Butter Gnocchi

Ingredients:

- 1 pound potato gnocchi (store-bought or homemade)
- 4 tablespoons truffle butter
- 2 tablespoons olive oil
- 2 cloves garlic, minced
- Salt and black pepper to taste
- Grated Parmesan cheese for serving (optional)
- Fresh parsley, chopped, for garnish

Instructions:

Cook Gnocchi:

- If using store-bought gnocchi, follow the package instructions for cooking. If making homemade gnocchi, boil them in salted water until they float to the surface, indicating they are cooked. Drain and set aside.

Prepare Truffle Butter Sauce:

- In a large skillet, melt truffle butter and olive oil over medium heat.

Sauté Garlic:

- Add minced garlic to the skillet and sauté for 1-2 minutes until fragrant. Be careful not to let the garlic brown.

Toss Gnocchi:

- Add the cooked and drained gnocchi to the skillet. Toss gently to coat the gnocchi evenly with the truffle butter sauce.

Season:

- Season the gnocchi with salt and black pepper to taste. Truffle butter already has a robust flavor, so adjust the seasoning according to your preference.

Serve:

- Transfer the truffle butter gnocchi to serving plates or a platter.

Garnish:

- Optionally, sprinkle grated Parmesan cheese over the gnocchi and garnish with chopped fresh parsley.

Enjoy:

- Serve the Truffle Butter Gnocchi immediately, savoring the rich and aromatic flavors.

This dish is simple yet elegant, allowing the earthy and luxurious taste of truffle to shine. You can customize it further by adding a touch of truffle salt or shaving some fresh truffle over the gnocchi for an extra indulgent experience. Pair it with a glass of white wine for a delightful culinary treat.

Wild Mushroom and Fontina Ravioli with Brown Butter Sauce

Ingredients:

- 1 pound wild mushroom and Fontina ravioli (store-bought or homemade)
- 1/2 cup unsalted butter
- 2 cloves garlic, minced
- 1/4 cup fresh sage leaves
- Salt and black pepper to taste
- Grated Parmesan cheese for serving
- Toasted pine nuts for garnish (optional)

Instructions:

Cook Ravioli:

- If using store-bought ravioli, follow the package instructions for cooking. If using homemade ravioli, boil them in salted water until they float to the surface, indicating they are cooked. Drain and set aside.

Prepare Brown Butter Sauce:

- In a large skillet, melt unsalted butter over medium heat. Allow the butter to cook until it turns a golden brown color. Be attentive to avoid burning the butter.

Add Garlic and Sage:

- Add minced garlic and fresh sage leaves to the browned butter. Sauté for 1-2 minutes until the garlic is fragrant, and the sage becomes crispy. Be careful not to burn the garlic.

Toss Ravioli:

- Add the cooked and drained wild mushroom and Fontina ravioli to the skillet. Gently toss the ravioli in the brown butter sauce, ensuring they are well coated.

Season:

- Season the ravioli with salt and black pepper to taste. The brown butter sauce adds a rich and nutty flavor, so adjust the seasoning according to your preference.

Serve:

- Transfer the ravioli to serving plates or a platter.

Garnish:

- Optionally, sprinkle grated Parmesan cheese over the ravioli and garnish with toasted pine nuts for an extra crunch and flavor.

Enjoy:

- Serve the Wild Mushroom and Fontina Ravioli with Brown Butter Sauce immediately, savoring the delightful combination of earthy mushrooms, creamy Fontina, and the nuttiness of brown butter.

This dish is perfect for a cozy dinner or a special occasion. The brown butter sauce enhances the flavors of the ravioli, making it a comforting and elegant pasta dish. Pair it with a light salad or a glass of white wine for a complete meal.

Wild Mushroom and Fontina Ravioli with Brown Butter Sauce

Ingredients:

- 1 pound wild mushroom and Fontina ravioli (store-bought or homemade)
- 1/2 cup unsalted butter
- 2 cloves garlic, minced
- 1/4 cup fresh sage leaves
- Salt and black pepper to taste
- Grated Parmesan cheese for serving
- Toasted pine nuts for garnish (optional)

Instructions:

Cook Ravioli:

- If using store-bought ravioli, follow the package instructions for cooking. If using homemade ravioli, boil them in salted water until they float to the surface, indicating they are cooked. Drain and set aside.

Prepare Brown Butter Sauce:

- In a large skillet, melt unsalted butter over medium heat. Allow the butter to cook until it turns a golden brown color. Be attentive to avoid burning the butter.

Add Garlic and Sage:

- Add minced garlic and fresh sage leaves to the browned butter. Sauté for 1-2 minutes until the garlic is fragrant, and the sage becomes crispy. Be careful not to burn the garlic.

Toss Ravioli:

- Add the cooked and drained wild mushroom and Fontina ravioli to the skillet. Gently toss the ravioli in the brown butter sauce, ensuring they are well coated.

Season:

- Season the ravioli with salt and black pepper to taste. The brown butter sauce adds a rich and nutty flavor, so adjust the seasoning according to your preference.

Serve:

- Transfer the ravioli to serving plates or a platter.

Garnish:

- Optionally, sprinkle grated Parmesan cheese over the ravioli and garnish with toasted pine nuts for an extra crunch and flavor.

Enjoy:

- Serve the Wild Mushroom and Fontina Ravioli with Brown Butter Sauce immediately, savoring the delightful combination of earthy mushrooms, creamy Fontina, and the nuttiness of brown butter.

This dish is perfect for a cozy dinner or a special occasion. The brown butter sauce enhances the flavors of the ravioli, making it a comforting and elegant pasta dish. Pair it with a light salad or a glass of white wine for a complete meal.

Pappardelle with Braised Short Rib Ragu

Ingredients:

For the Braised Short Ribs:

- 2 pounds bone-in beef short ribs
- Salt and black pepper to taste
- 2 tablespoons olive oil
- 1 onion, finely chopped
- 2 carrots, peeled and diced
- 2 celery stalks, diced
- 4 cloves garlic, minced
- 1 cup red wine
- 2 cups beef broth
- 1 can (14 ounces) crushed tomatoes
- 2 bay leaves
- 1 teaspoon dried thyme
- 1 teaspoon dried rosemary

For the Pasta:

- 1 pound pappardelle pasta
- Salt for boiling water

For Finishing:

- Grated Parmesan cheese for serving
- Fresh parsley, chopped, for garnish

Instructions:

For the Braised Short Ribs:

Preheat Oven:
- Preheat your oven to 325°F (163°C).

Season Short Ribs:
- Season the short ribs with salt and black pepper.

Brown Short Ribs:
- In a large oven-safe Dutch oven, heat olive oil over medium-high heat. Brown the short ribs on all sides. Remove them from the pot and set aside.

Sauté Vegetables:
- In the same pot, add chopped onion, diced carrots, diced celery, and minced garlic. Sauté until the vegetables are softened.

Deglaze with Wine:
- Pour in the red wine to deglaze the pot, scraping up any browned bits from the bottom.

Add Remaining Ingredients:
- Return the browned short ribs to the pot. Add beef broth, crushed tomatoes, bay leaves, dried thyme, and dried rosemary.

Braise in Oven:
- Cover the pot and transfer it to the preheated oven. Braise for 2.5 to 3 hours or until the short ribs are fork-tender.

Shred Meat:
- Once the short ribs are cooked, remove them from the pot and shred the meat, discarding any bones and excess fat. Return the shredded meat to the sauce.

For the Pasta:

Cook Pappardelle:

- Cook the pappardelle pasta in a large pot of salted boiling water according to the package instructions. Drain.

Combine Pasta and Ragu:

- Toss the cooked pappardelle in the braised short rib ragu, ensuring the pasta is well coated with the rich sauce.

Serve:

- Divide the Pappardelle with Braised Short Rib Ragu among serving plates.

Garnish:

- Sprinkle grated Parmesan cheese over each serving and garnish with chopped fresh parsley.

Enjoy:

- Serve immediately, savoring the hearty and comforting flavors of this delicious pasta dish.

Pappardelle with Braised Short Rib Ragu is a satisfying meal that's perfect for special occasions or a cozy dinner. The slow-cooked short ribs infuse the sauce with rich flavors, making it a standout dish. Pair it with a robust red wine for a delightful dining experience.

Lemon and Shrimp Scampi Linguine

Ingredients:

- 1 pound linguine pasta
- 1 pound large shrimp, peeled and deveined
- Salt and black pepper to taste
- 3 tablespoons olive oil
- 4 cloves garlic, minced
- 1/2 teaspoon red pepper flakes (optional for a bit of heat)
- Zest of 2 lemons
- Juice of 2 lemons
- 1/2 cup dry white wine
- 1/2 cup chicken or vegetable broth
- 1/4 cup fresh parsley, chopped
- Grated Parmesan cheese for serving

Instructions:

Cook Linguine:

- Cook the linguine pasta in a large pot of salted boiling water according to the package instructions. Drain and set aside.

Season Shrimp:

- Season the shrimp with salt and black pepper.

Sauté Shrimp:

- In a large skillet, heat 2 tablespoons of olive oil over medium-high heat. Add the seasoned shrimp and cook until they turn pink, about 2-3 minutes per side. Remove the shrimp from the skillet and set aside.

Make Lemon and Garlic Sauce:

- In the same skillet, add the remaining 1 tablespoon of olive oil. Add minced garlic and red pepper flakes (if using). Sauté for about 1 minute until the garlic is fragrant.

Deglaze with Wine and Broth:

- Pour in the dry white wine to deglaze the skillet, scraping up any browned bits from the bottom. Add chicken or vegetable broth, lemon zest, and lemon juice. Allow the mixture to simmer for 2-3 minutes.

Return Shrimp:

- Return the cooked shrimp to the skillet and toss them in the lemony sauce.

Add Linguine and Parsley:

- Add the cooked linguine to the skillet and toss everything together, ensuring the pasta is well coated in the flavorful sauce. Add chopped fresh parsley and toss again.

Adjust Seasoning:

- Taste and adjust the seasoning with salt and black pepper as needed.

Serve:

- Divide the Lemon and Shrimp Scampi Linguine among serving plates.

Garnish:

- Garnish with grated Parmesan cheese and additional fresh parsley.

Enjoy:

- Serve immediately, savoring the bright and zesty flavors of this delightful shrimp scampi linguine.

This Lemon and Shrimp Scampi Linguine is a light and vibrant dish that's perfect for a quick weeknight dinner or a special occasion. The combination of lemon, garlic, and shrimp creates a mouthwatering flavor profile that's sure to be a hit. Pair it with a glass of crisp white wine for a complete meal.

Vegetarian

Eggplant Parmesan Tower with Fresh Tomato Sauce

Ingredients:

For the Eggplant:

- 2 large eggplants, thinly sliced into rounds
- Salt for sweating eggplant
- Olive oil for brushing eggplant
- 1 cup all-purpose flour
- 2 large eggs, beaten
- 2 cups breadcrumbs (seasoned with salt, pepper, and dried herbs)
- Vegetable oil for frying

For the Fresh Tomato Sauce:

- 4 large tomatoes, diced
- 3 cloves garlic, minced
- 1/4 cup fresh basil, chopped
- Salt and black pepper to taste
- 2 tablespoons olive oil

For Assembling:

- Mozzarella cheese, shredded
- Parmesan cheese, grated
- Fresh basil leaves for garnish

Instructions:

For the Eggplant:

Sweat and Drain Eggplant:

- Lay the eggplant slices on a tray, sprinkle with salt, and let them sit for about 30 minutes to sweat. Afterward, pat them dry with a paper towel to remove excess moisture.

Coat Eggplant:

- Dredge each eggplant slice in flour, dip in beaten eggs, and coat with seasoned breadcrumbs.

Fry Eggplant:

- In a large skillet, heat vegetable oil over medium-high heat. Fry the breaded eggplant slices until golden brown on both sides. Place them on a paper towel-lined plate to absorb excess oil.

For the Fresh Tomato Sauce:

Make Sauce:

- In a saucepan, heat olive oil over medium heat. Add minced garlic and sauté until fragrant. Add diced tomatoes, chopped basil, salt, and black pepper. Simmer for about 15-20 minutes until the sauce thickens.

For Assembling the Eggplant Parmesan Tower:

Preheat Oven:

- Preheat your oven to 375°F (190°C).

Layer Components:

- In a baking dish, start assembling the towers by layering fried eggplant slices, a spoonful of fresh tomato sauce, and a sprinkle of shredded mozzarella and grated Parmesan. Repeat until you have a tower-like structure.

Top with Cheese:

- Finish the towers with a generous amount of shredded mozzarella and grated Parmesan on top.

Bake:

- Bake in the preheated oven for about 20-25 minutes or until the cheese is melted and bubbly, and the eggplant is cooked through.

Garnish:

- Garnish with fresh basil leaves just before serving.

Serve:

- Serve each Eggplant Parmesan Tower on individual plates, and drizzle with additional fresh tomato sauce if desired.

Enjoy:

- Enjoy the Eggplant Parmesan Tower with Fresh Tomato Sauce as a delicious and visually stunning main course!

This Eggplant Parmesan Tower is a fantastic way to showcase the flavors of eggplant and fresh tomato sauce. The crispy and golden brown exterior of the eggplant layers, combined with the gooey melted cheese and aromatic tomato sauce, makes it a delightful and satisfying dish.

Quinoa-Stuffed Bell Peppers with Feta and Spinach

Ingredients:

- 4 large bell peppers, halved and seeds removed
- 1 cup quinoa, rinsed
- 2 cups vegetable broth or water
- 1 tablespoon olive oil
- 1 onion, finely chopped
- 2 cloves garlic, minced
- 2 cups fresh spinach, chopped
- 1 cup cherry tomatoes, halved
- 1/2 cup crumbled feta cheese
- 1 teaspoon dried oregano
- Salt and black pepper to taste
- Fresh parsley, chopped, for garnish

Instructions:

Preheat Oven:

- Preheat your oven to 375°F (190°C).

Prepare Bell Peppers:

- Cut the bell peppers in half lengthwise and remove the seeds and membranes. Place the pepper halves in a baking dish.

Cook Quinoa:

- In a saucepan, combine the quinoa and vegetable broth or water. Bring to a boil, then reduce the heat to low, cover, and simmer for about 15 minutes or until the quinoa is cooked and the liquid is absorbed. Fluff the quinoa with a fork.

Sauté Onion and Garlic:

- In a large skillet, heat olive oil over medium heat. Add chopped onion and sauté until translucent. Add minced garlic and cook for an additional minute.

Add Spinach and Tomatoes:
- Add chopped spinach to the skillet and cook until wilted. Stir in halved cherry tomatoes and cook for another 2 minutes.

Combine Quinoa and Vegetables:
- Transfer the cooked quinoa to the skillet with sautéed vegetables. Mix well to combine.

Season and Add Feta:
- Season the quinoa and vegetable mixture with dried oregano, salt, and black pepper. Add crumbled feta cheese and stir until everything is well combined.

Stuff Bell Peppers:
- Spoon the quinoa and vegetable mixture into each bell pepper half, pressing down gently to pack the stuffing.

Bake:
- Cover the baking dish with aluminum foil and bake in the preheated oven for 25-30 minutes, or until the bell peppers are tender.

Garnish and Serve:
- Remove from the oven, garnish with chopped fresh parsley, and serve the Quinoa-Stuffed Bell Peppers with Feta and Spinach.

Enjoy:
- Enjoy these wholesome and flavorful stuffed peppers as a delicious and nutritious meal!

These Quinoa-Stuffed Bell Peppers are not only a feast for the eyes but also a nutritious and satisfying dish. The combination of quinoa, feta, spinach, and tomatoes creates a delicious and well-balanced flavor profile. Feel free to customize the recipe by adding your favorite herbs or spices to suit your taste preferences.

Butternut Squash and Sage Risotto

Ingredients:

- 1 small butternut squash, peeled, seeded, and diced into small cubes
- 2 tablespoons olive oil
- Salt and black pepper to taste
- 1 cup Arborio rice
- 1/2 cup dry white wine
- 4 cups vegetable broth, kept warm
- 1 onion, finely chopped
- 2 cloves garlic, minced
- 1/4 cup fresh sage leaves, chopped
- 1/2 cup Parmesan cheese, grated
- 2 tablespoons unsalted butter
- Optional: Extra sage leaves for garnish

Instructions:

Roast Butternut Squash:

- Preheat your oven to 400°F (200°C). Place the diced butternut squash on a baking sheet, drizzle with olive oil, and season with salt and black pepper. Roast in the oven for about 25-30 minutes or until the squash is tender and slightly caramelized.

Prepare Risotto Base:

- In a large skillet or saucepan, heat 1 tablespoon of olive oil over medium heat. Add the chopped onion and sauté until softened.

Toast Rice:

- Add the Arborio rice to the skillet and cook, stirring, for 1-2 minutes until the rice is lightly toasted.

Deglaze with Wine:

- Pour in the dry white wine, stirring constantly until most of the wine is absorbed.

Add Sage and Garlic:

- Add minced garlic and chopped sage leaves to the rice. Sauté for an additional 1-2 minutes until the sage becomes fragrant.

Begin Adding Broth:

- Begin adding the warm vegetable broth, one ladle at a time, stirring frequently. Allow the liquid to be mostly absorbed before adding the next ladle of broth. Continue this process until the rice is creamy and cooked to al dente texture. This should take about 18-20 minutes.

Incorporate Butternut Squash:

- About halfway through the cooking process, stir in the roasted butternut squash cubes.

Finish Risotto:

- Once the rice is cooked, stir in grated Parmesan cheese and unsalted butter. Season with salt and black pepper to taste.

Garnish and Serve:

- Garnish the Butternut Squash and Sage Risotto with extra sage leaves if desired.

Enjoy:

- Serve the risotto immediately, savoring the creamy texture and the delightful combination of butternut squash and sage.

This Butternut Squash and Sage Risotto is a comforting dish that makes a perfect fall or winter meal. The sweet and nutty flavor of the roasted butternut squash complements the earthy sage, creating a harmonious and satisfying dish. Serve it as a main course or as a side dish alongside your favorite protein.

Wild Mushroom and Spinach Stuffed Portobello Mushrooms

Ingredients:

- 4 large portobello mushrooms, stems removed
- 2 tablespoons olive oil
- 1 onion, finely chopped
- 2 cloves garlic, minced
- 2 cups wild mushrooms (such as shiitake, oyster, or cremini), chopped
- 2 cups fresh spinach, chopped
- Salt and black pepper to taste
- 1/2 cup breadcrumbs
- 1/2 cup grated Parmesan cheese
- 1/4 cup fresh parsley, chopped
- 1/4 cup pine nuts (optional for added crunch)
- 1/4 cup feta cheese, crumbled (optional for extra creaminess)

Instructions:

Preheat Oven:

- Preheat your oven to 375°F (190°C).

Prepare Portobello Mushrooms:

- Clean the portobello mushrooms and remove the stems. Place them on a baking sheet.

Sauté Onion and Garlic:

- In a skillet, heat olive oil over medium heat. Add finely chopped onion and sauté until softened. Add minced garlic and cook for an additional 1-2 minutes.

Cook Wild Mushrooms:

- Add the chopped wild mushrooms to the skillet and cook until they release their moisture and become tender.

Add Spinach:

- Stir in the chopped fresh spinach and cook until wilted. Season the mixture with salt and black pepper to taste.

Prepare Filling:

- In a bowl, combine the sautéed mushroom and spinach mixture with breadcrumbs, grated Parmesan cheese, fresh parsley, and pine nuts (if using). Mix well. If desired, add crumbled feta cheese for extra creaminess.

Stuff Portobello Mushrooms:

- Spoon the filling into each portobello mushroom cap, pressing down gently to pack the stuffing.

Bake:

- Bake in the preheated oven for about 20-25 minutes, or until the mushrooms are tender and the stuffing is golden brown.

Garnish:

- Garnish with additional fresh parsley and a sprinkle of Parmesan cheese before serving.

Enjoy:

- Serve the Wild Mushroom and Spinach Stuffed Portobello Mushrooms as an appetizer or a light meal, savoring the rich and savory flavors.

These stuffed portobello mushrooms are not only delicious but also versatile. You can customize the filling with your favorite herbs, cheeses, or additional vegetables. Enjoy them on their own or as a side dish for a wholesome and flavorful experience.

Vegetarian Moussaka

Ingredients:

For the Filling:

- 1 cup dry lentils, rinsed
- 3 cups water
- 2 tablespoons olive oil
- 1 onion, finely chopped
- 3 cloves garlic, minced
- 1 can (14 ounces) crushed tomatoes
- 1 teaspoon dried oregano
- 1 teaspoon dried thyme
- Salt and black pepper to taste

For the Vegetables:

- 2 large eggplants, sliced into rounds
- 2 zucchinis, sliced into rounds
- Olive oil for brushing
- Salt and black pepper to taste

For the Béchamel Sauce:

- 1/4 cup unsalted butter
- 1/4 cup all-purpose flour
- 2 cups milk
- Salt and nutmeg to taste

- 1 cup grated Parmesan cheese

Instructions:

For the Lentil Filling:

  Cook Lentils:
  - In a saucepan, combine the dry lentils and water. Bring to a boil, then reduce the heat to low, cover, and simmer for about 20-25 minutes or until the lentils are tender. Drain any excess water.

  Sauté Onion and Garlic:
  - In a large skillet, heat olive oil over medium heat. Add finely chopped onion and sauté until softened. Add minced garlic and cook for an additional 1-2 minutes.

  Add Tomatoes and Lentils:
  - Stir in crushed tomatoes, cooked lentils, dried oregano, dried thyme, salt, and black pepper. Simmer for 10-15 minutes, allowing the flavors to meld. Adjust seasoning if needed.

For the Vegetables:

  Preheat Oven:
  - Preheat your oven to 375°F (190°C).

  Roast Eggplant and Zucchini:
  - Arrange the eggplant and zucchini slices on baking sheets. Brush with olive oil and season with salt and black pepper. Roast in the preheated oven for about 20-25 minutes or until tender.

For the Béchamel Sauce:

Make Roux:

- In a saucepan, melt butter over medium heat. Add all-purpose flour and whisk continuously to form a roux.

Add Milk:

- Gradually add milk to the roux, whisking constantly to avoid lumps. Continue cooking until the sauce thickens.

Season and Add Cheese:

- Season the béchamel sauce with salt and nutmeg. Stir in grated Parmesan cheese until smooth and well combined. Remove from heat.

Assembling Moussaka:

Layer Vegetables and Filling:

- In a baking dish, layer the roasted eggplant and zucchini slices. Top with the lentil and tomato filling.

Pour Béchamel Sauce:

- Pour the béchamel sauce over the lentil filling, spreading it evenly.

Bake:

- Bake in the preheated oven for about 30-35 minutes or until the top is golden brown.

Rest and Serve:

- Allow the Vegetarian Moussaka to rest for a few minutes before slicing. Serve warm.

Enjoy:

- Enjoy the layers of flavor and texture in this delicious Vegetarian Moussaka!

This vegetarian twist on Moussaka provides a hearty and satisfying meal without the meat. The combination of lentils, roasted vegetables, and creamy béchamel sauce creates a flavorful and comforting dish. Serve it with a side salad or crusty bread for a complete meal.

Side Dishes:

Truffle Mashed Potatoes

Ingredients:
- 4 large russet potatoes, peeled and cut into chunks
- 4 tablespoons unsalted butter
- 1/2 cup heavy cream
- Salt and white pepper to taste
- 2 tablespoons truffle oil
- 2 tablespoons fresh chives, chopped (for garnish, optional)

Instructions:

Boil Potatoes:
- Place the potato chunks in a large pot and cover them with cold water. Bring the water to a boil and cook the potatoes until they are fork-tender, about 15-20 minutes.

Drain and Mash:
- Drain the potatoes and return them to the pot. Mash the potatoes using a potato masher or a ricer until smooth.

Add Butter and Cream:
- While the potatoes are still hot, add the unsalted butter and heavy cream. Mix until the butter is melted, and the cream is fully incorporated.

Season:
- Season the mashed potatoes with salt and white pepper to taste. White pepper is often preferred in truffle dishes to maintain the visual appeal, but black pepper can be used if you prefer.

Add Truffle Oil:

- Drizzle in the truffle oil and fold it into the mashed potatoes. Truffle oil is potent, so start with a small amount, taste, and add more if desired.

Adjust Consistency:

- If the mashed potatoes are too thick, you can add more cream until you reach your desired consistency.

Garnish:

- Garnish the Truffle Mashed Potatoes with chopped fresh chives if desired for a pop of color and added freshness.

Serve:

- Serve the Truffle Mashed Potatoes warm, and enjoy the rich and decadent flavors.

Note:

- Truffle oil can vary in intensity, so it's advisable to start with a small amount and add more to taste. You can always adjust the quantity based on your preference.

Truffle Mashed Potatoes are an excellent side dish for special occasions or when you want to add a touch of elegance to your meal. The truffle oil infuses the dish with a distinct and indulgent flavor, making it a delightful complement to various main courses.

Grilled Asparagus with Lemon Zest and Parmesan

Ingredients:

- 1 bunch of fresh asparagus, tough ends trimmed
- 2 tablespoons olive oil
- Salt and black pepper to taste
- Zest of 1 lemon
- 1/4 cup Parmesan cheese, shaved or grated
- Fresh lemon wedges for serving

Instructions:

Preheat Grill:

- Preheat your grill to medium-high heat.

Prepare Asparagus:

- Wash and trim the tough ends from the asparagus spears.

Coat with Olive Oil:

- Place the trimmed asparagus in a bowl and drizzle with olive oil. Toss to coat the asparagus evenly.

Season:

- Season the asparagus with salt and black pepper to taste. Toss again to ensure even seasoning.

Grill Asparagus:

- Lay the asparagus spears on the preheated grill. Grill for about 3-5 minutes, turning occasionally, until the asparagus is tender and has a nice grill mark.

Zest Lemon:

- While the asparagus is grilling, zest one lemon. Be careful to only grate the yellow part of the peel, avoiding the bitter white pith.

Plate Asparagus:

- Arrange the grilled asparagus on a serving platter.

Sprinkle Lemon Zest and Parmesan:

- Sprinkle the lemon zest over the grilled asparagus. Top with shaved or grated Parmesan cheese.

Serve:

- Serve the Grilled Asparagus with Lemon Zest and Parmesan immediately, with additional lemon wedges on the side for squeezing.

Enjoy:

- Enjoy this flavorful and vibrant side dish that beautifully combines the smokiness of grilled asparagus with the brightness of lemon zest and the richness of Parmesan.

This Grilled Asparagus with Lemon Zest and Parmesan is not only a visually appealing side dish but also a perfect way to highlight the natural freshness of asparagus. The combination of the charred asparagus, zesty lemon, and savory Parmesan creates a well-balanced and delightful flavor profile. It pairs well with a variety of main courses and is especially fitting for spring and summer meals.

Cauliflower Gratin with Gruyere

Ingredients:

- 1 large head of cauliflower, cut into florets
- 3 tablespoons unsalted butter
- 3 tablespoons all-purpose flour
- 2 cups whole milk
- 2 cups Gruyere cheese, shredded
- 1/2 cup Parmesan cheese, grated
- Salt and black pepper to taste
- 1/4 teaspoon nutmeg (freshly grated, if possible)
- 1/2 cup breadcrumbs (optional, for topping)
- Fresh parsley, chopped (for garnish)

Instructions:

Preheat Oven:

- Preheat your oven to 375°F (190°C).

Steam Cauliflower:

- Steam the cauliflower florets until they are just tender. This can be done by placing them in a steamer basket over boiling water for about 5-7 minutes.

Prepare Cheese Sauce:

- In a saucepan, melt the butter over medium heat. Stir in the flour to create a roux. Cook the roux for 1-2 minutes, stirring continuously.

Add Milk:

- Gradually whisk in the whole milk, making sure there are no lumps. Continue to whisk until the mixture thickens.

Add Gruyere and Parmesan:

- Reduce the heat to low. Add the shredded Gruyere and grated Parmesan to the sauce. Stir until the cheese is fully melted and the sauce is smooth.

Season:

- Season the cheese sauce with salt, black pepper, and freshly grated nutmeg. Adjust the seasoning according to your taste.

Combine with Cauliflower:

- Gently fold the steamed cauliflower into the cheese sauce until the cauliflower is well-coated.

Transfer to Baking Dish:

- Transfer the cauliflower and cheese mixture to a greased baking dish, spreading it out evenly.

Optional Breadcrumb Topping:

- If desired, sprinkle breadcrumbs evenly over the cauliflower mixture for a golden and crispy topping.

Bake:

- Bake in the preheated oven for approximately 25-30 minutes or until the cauliflower is tender, and the top is golden and bubbly.

Garnish and Serve:

- Garnish the Cauliflower Gratin with Gruyere with chopped fresh parsley before serving.

Enjoy:

- Serve this decadent Cauliflower Gratin as a delightful side dish, savoring the creamy texture and the rich flavor of Gruyere.

This Cauliflower Gratin with Gruyere is a wonderful way to turn cauliflower into a comforting and elegant dish. The creamy Gruyere cheese sauce elevates the cauliflower to a whole new level of deliciousness. It's perfect for holiday dinners, special occasions, or whenever you want to enjoy a comforting and cheesy side dish.

Roasted Brussels Sprouts with Balsamic Glaze and Bacon

Ingredients:

- 1 pound Brussels sprouts, trimmed and halved
- 3 tablespoons olive oil
- Salt and black pepper to taste
- 4 slices bacon, cooked and crumbled
- 2 tablespoons balsamic glaze
- 1 tablespoon honey (optional, for added sweetness)
- 2 tablespoons chopped fresh parsley (for garnish)

Instructions:

Preheat Oven:

- Preheat your oven to 400°F (200°C).

Prepare Brussels Sprouts:

- Trim the ends of the Brussels sprouts and cut them in half. Place them in a large mixing bowl.

Coat with Olive Oil:

- Drizzle the Brussels sprouts with olive oil and toss them to coat evenly. Season with salt and black pepper to taste.

Roast Brussels Sprouts:

- Spread the Brussels sprouts on a baking sheet in a single layer. Roast in the preheated oven for 20-25 minutes or until they are golden brown and crispy on the edges, tossing halfway through for even roasting.

Cook Bacon:

- While the Brussels sprouts are roasting, cook the bacon until it's crispy. Once cooked, crumble the bacon into small pieces.

Toss with Bacon and Balsamic Glaze:

- In a large bowl, combine the roasted Brussels sprouts with the crumbled bacon. Drizzle with balsamic glaze and toss to coat. If you prefer a touch of sweetness, you can also drizzle honey over the mixture and toss again.

Garnish:

- Garnish the Roasted Brussels Sprouts with Balsamic Glaze and Bacon with chopped fresh parsley for a burst of freshness.

Serve:

- Serve the dish warm as a flavorful and satisfying side.

Enjoy:

- Enjoy the combination of crispy Brussels sprouts, savory bacon, and sweet balsamic glaze in this delightful side dish.

This recipe creates a perfect balance of flavors and textures, making it an excellent side dish for various occasions. The balsamic glaze adds a touch of sweetness, complementing the smokiness of the bacon and the caramelized Brussels sprouts. It's a crowd-pleaser that pairs well with a variety of main courses.

Wild Rice Pilaf with Pomegranate Seeds and Pistachios

Ingredients:

- 1 cup wild rice, rinsed
- 2 1/2 cups vegetable or chicken broth
- 1 tablespoon olive oil
- 1 onion, finely chopped
- 2 cloves garlic, minced
- 1/2 cup chopped celery
- 1/2 cup chopped carrots
- 1/2 cup chopped mushrooms
- 1/2 teaspoon dried thyme
- Salt and black pepper to taste
- 1/2 cup pomegranate seeds
- 1/3 cup chopped pistachios
- Fresh parsley, chopped (for garnish)

Instructions:

Cook Wild Rice:

- In a medium saucepan, combine the rinsed wild rice and vegetable or chicken broth. Bring to a boil, then reduce the heat to low, cover, and simmer for about 40-45 minutes or until the rice is tender and has absorbed the liquid. Fluff the rice with a fork.

Sauté Vegetables:

- In a large skillet, heat olive oil over medium heat. Add the chopped onion, garlic, celery, carrots, and mushrooms. Sauté until the vegetables are softened.

Add Thyme and Season:
- Stir in the dried thyme and season with salt and black pepper to taste. Cook for an additional 2-3 minutes.

Combine Rice and Vegetables:
- Add the cooked wild rice to the skillet with the sautéed vegetables. Stir to combine and let the flavors meld for a few minutes.

Fold in Pomegranate Seeds and Pistachios:
- Gently fold in the pomegranate seeds and chopped pistachios, reserving some for garnish. The vibrant colors and textures add a festive touch.

Garnish and Serve:
- Garnish the Wild Rice Pilaf with additional pomegranate seeds, pistachios, and chopped fresh parsley.

Serve Warm:
- Serve the Wild Rice Pilaf with Pomegranate Seeds and Pistachios warm as a delightful and visually appealing side dish.

Enjoy:
- Enjoy the unique combination of flavors and textures in this festive wild rice pilaf.

This Wild Rice Pilaf is not only delicious but also adds a burst of color and elegance to your table. The sweetness of pomegranate seeds and the crunch of pistachios complement the nutty wild rice, creating a dish that's perfect for holiday gatherings or special occasions.